Books by David D. Wilson

A Study on the Holy Ghost
A Study on the Three Johns
The Revelation of Jesus Christ
A Study on the Warnings of Jude
A Study on the Two Peters
A Study on the Book of James
A Study on Titus and Philemon

Order your copy at:

www.ParadiseGospelPress.com

or contact us at

Paradise Gospel Press
P.O. Box 184
Paradise, Texas 76073

A Study on Titus & Philemon

Rev. David D. Wilson

PARADISE GOSPEL PRESS

A STUDY ON TITUS & PHILEMON,
Wilson, David D.

First Edition

To Be Like Jesus by L.R. Ooton (1923) – Public Domain
Amazing Grace by John Newton (1779) – Public Domain

PARADISE GOSPEL PRESS

www.paradisegospelpress.com

ISBN: 978-1-946823-06-9

Table of Contents

Titus

Philemon

Bibliography

Answers

The Book of

Titus

Introduction to Titus

Who was Titus? Nothing is known about Titus except what we find in the New Testament. Titus was Greek, so it is certain he was uncircumcised. He lived like other Greeks until his conversion. The year Titus first met Paul and heard him preach is unknown.

As for his salvation, it was before the fourteenth year of Paul's conversion, since Titus was with Paul in Jerusalem, already a Christian and a follower of Jesus Christ. While there, the revelation that Gentile Christians did not have to follow Jewish customs and traditions concerning circumcision and dietary laws to be a follower of Jesus Christ was confirmed.

We know that after the council at Jerusalem, Titus accompanied Paul and Barnabas and attended to the apostles' needs for a time while preaching the gospel message. In II Corinthians 7:6, Paul writes about Titus.

II Corinthians 7:6

Nevertheless God, that comforteth those that are

cast down, comforted us by the coming of Titus;

As we read the scriptures, we can plainly see that Titus was very important to Paul's ministry. One reason was because Titus was a comfort to Paul while in Corinth.

II Corinthians 2:13

I had no rest in my spirit, because I found not Titus my brother: but taking my leave of them, I went from thence into Macedonia.

II Corinthians 7:6, 13

⁶ Nevertheless God, that comforteth those that are cast down, comforted us by the coming of Titus; ¹³ Therefore we were comforted in your comfort: yea, and exceedingly the more joyed we for the joy of Titus, because his spirit was refreshed by you all.

II Corinthians 12:18

I desired Titus, and with him I sent a brother. Did Titus make a gain of you? walked we not in the same spirit? walked we not in the same steps?

Titus was a trusted and very confident laborer with Paul in the ministry of God's work, so much so that Paul left Titus on the island of Crete to set in order the things that were in disarray. He was also to ordain elders in all of the cities around about Crete (and the neighboring islands). All of this took place around the year A.D. 62.

We know that Titus was with Paul in Rome the second time while Paul was imprisoned. Titus left Paul to go to Dalmatia before Paul's trial, after which there is no further record of Titus. However, tradition has it that Titus went back to the island of Crete and preached to the Cretians (Cretans) and to the people on the surrounding islands.

According to tradition, Titus died on Crete at the old age of ninety-four years.

Chapter 1

Titus 1:1-4

¹ Paul, a servant of God, and an apostle of Jesus
Christ, according to the faith of God's elect, and the
acknowledging of the truth which is after godliness;
² In hope of eternal life, which God, that cannot lie,
promised before the world began;
³ But hath in due times manifested his word through
preaching, which is committed unto me according
to the commandment of God our Saviour;
⁴ To Titus, mine own son after the common faith:
Grace, mercy, and peace, from God the Father and
the Lord Jesus Christ our Saviour.

In this first verse, Paul declares who he is, **an apostle of Jesus Christ called of God to proclaim the gospel** of salvation before a lost and dying world. Paul, as we know, was **a man of faith, a true believer**. He was what we all strive to be, **one of God's chosen elect**. He acknowledges the power and the truth that is in Jesus

Christ, our Lord. He acknowledges that **Jesus is our one and only Saviour and Redeemer**, and that Jesus is the only redeemer for all of mankind.

Paul believed in living a life of **holiness and godliness before this present world**. He was our model showing that as we give ourselves to Jesus, He begins to **change us from the inside out**. He teaches us by example that we can **stand upon the promises in God's Holy Word**, for as the scriptures teach, God cannot lie. God established His Precious Holy Word before the beginning of this world.

2 Corinthians 7:1

> *Having therefore these promises, dearly beloved, let us cleanse ourselves from all filthiness of the flesh and spirit, perfecting holiness in the fear of God.*

2 Peter 1:3-4

> *³ According as his divine power hath given unto us all things that pertain unto life and godliness, through the knowledge of him that hath called us to glory and virtue:*
> *⁴ Whereby are given unto us exceeding great and precious promises: that by these ye might be partakers of the divine nature, having escaped the corruption that is in the world through lust.*

The promises of God are eternal; they are for His children, the saints. Like Paul, we can **live by them and stand upon them**, because God will **never fail those who live for Him** and serve Him.

As we look at verse three, Paul states that God "*in due times*" has **manifested Himself through the preaching of His Holy Word**. This commission was given to Paul on the Damascus road, **to preach the unsearchable riches of God's glory, so that the lost souls of this world might be saved**.

1 Corinthians 1:21

> *For after that in the wisdom of God the world by wisdom knew not God, it pleased God by the foolishness of preaching to save them that believe.*

The preaching of the gospel is a **very special calling put upon certain individuals** by God. Paul was such a person along with the other apostles. In God's plan, He has chosen **certain individuals, men and women**, to fill special positions in the work of reaching the lost. Some He calls to be ministers, some to be teachers and some to be missionaries. Whatever the calling may be, God will **give grace and power for you** to see your calling through.

God has a **plan for our lives**. He has seasons or times when we are to **step up and do what God wants done**. Our timing may not be God's timing; however, **always wait upon God's time**. Never get ahead of God; if you do, then you are out there by yourself. Likewise, neither let us lag behind God. We must **move with God to be profitable**, for to **everything there is a season and a time**. In Ecclesiastes, we read the writings of Solomon.

Ecclesiastes 3:1-8

> ¹ *To every thing there is a season, and a time to every purpose under the heaven:*
> ² *A time to be born, and a time to die; a time to plant, and a time to pluck up that which is planted;*
> ³ *A time to kill, and a time to heal; a time to break down, and a time to build up;*
> ⁴ *A time to weep, and a time to laugh; a time to mourn, and a time to dance;*
> ⁵ *A time to cast away stones, and a time to gather stones together; a time to embrace, and a time to refrain from embracing;*
> ⁶ *A time to get, and a time to lose; a time to keep, and a time to cast away;*
> ⁷ *A time to rend, and a time to sew; a time to keep silence, and a time to speak;*
> ⁸ *A time to love, and a time to hate; a time of war, and a time of peace.*

Just as it states in verse one, *"To every thing there is a season, and a time to every purpose under the heaven."* **God has a plan for our lives if we will live for Him.** That plan is to spread God's Word to the lost or sinners of this sinful world, whether **through preaching or witnessing to those who live around us**.

In verse four, Paul speaks of Titus as being his own son after the common faith. Was Titus Paul's son? Not in the natural; however, he was in the spiritual because it was **Paul who led Titus to Jesus Christ**. Paul's use of "*after the common*" means that we all are **saved or brought into the same faith by our belief in Jesus Christ** as our personal Saviour and Lord. This is the faith that all born-again believers have in common, a faith **common to each other**. This faith has no denominational labels; it is the **same for everyone who has been saved**. When we are born again, we all have this faith in common. It matters not what denomination you belong to: Baptist, Methodist, Church of Christ, Pentecostal or whatever you may be. We all must **be born again to enter into the common faith**.

Titus 1:5-9

[5] For this cause left I thee in Crete, that thou shouldest set in order the things that are wanting, and ordain elders in every city, as I had appointed thee:
[6] If any be blameless, the husband of one wife, having faithful children not accused of riot or unruly.
[7] For a bishop must be blameless, as the steward of God; not selfwilled, not soon angry, not given to wine, no striker, not given to filthy lucre;

*⁸ But a lover of hospitality, a lover of good men,
sober, just, holy, temperate;
⁹ Holding fast the faithful word as he hath been
taught, that he may be able by sound doctrine both
to exhort and to convince the gainsayers.*

Paul tells Titus why he left him in Crete in verse five. As we read, we are given to understand that there were problems in the local churches or assemblies. Paul **appointed Titus to act as he would act if he had stayed** in Crete. With this authority, Titus was to **set in order the things that they were wanting or missing**. These churches had not officially been set in a good working order. Some were not much more than prayer meetings with no official head or leaders.

Every assembly must have a form of leadership that is **scripturally sound in doctrine**. Not too much is known about how the services of the early church were run. Did they have a Sunday school? Likely not. In the early churches, the emphasis was upon **teaching the gospel message to everyone who would listen**. Yet the church must be more than a social gathering. There must be **rules of conduct and rules of order** for the church to follow. Along with this, there must be **elders ordained in every church**. Therefore, Titus was left **to attend to the work of setting each congregation in order**. The elders were men that were then given the responsibility of overseeing the church and its functions. Titus had to **get to know these men so that he would know their reputations**, their manners and how they ran their households to be sure that they were **worthy of the office to be put upon them**. God is **very particular who holds offices in His church**.

With verse seven, we begin to see the rules Titus was to go by. First, the elders **must have a blameless reputation**. In other words, there could be **no accusations of bad conduct** leveled against them. Second, they must be **the husband of one wife**. Contrary to what many believe, this does not mean that a divorced man could not fill the office of an elder. We need to use some common sense here. In the time of the early church, it was common for men to have more than one wife. Even in the Jewish law, if a man married and something happened to him so that he and his wife were childless at the time of his death, then one of his brothers was to take his widow to be his wife. The first child born to this union was to inherit the dead brother's estate. Thus, plural marriages were common among the Jewish people as well as the Gentiles. Just as today, there are places where plural marriages are lawful and widely accepted. Think about it, if a man in the early church had more than one wife and had children by them, and he came to the Lord and was saved, would it be right for him to divorce all his wives and their children except for one wife and her children? It would not be right for him to do this. You will not find in the scriptures any place where God specifically states that a man cannot have more than one wife. In most of this world's countries, plural marriages are illegal, however not in all of them. There are fifty-eight countries where plural marriages are legal out of the two hundred countries worldwide at the time this book was written. Therefore, the scripture means just what it says. The scripture is merely saying that **to hold the office of an elder, a man could only have one wife**.

To be an elder, a man can **only be married to one woman at a time**. If he has any children, they must also be faithful. Faithful children, according to what some commentators say, mean that all the children living at home must be saved, that they must be Christians. I do not necessarily agree with that statement, since a father cannot make his children accept the Lord as their Saviour. He lives a life before them as an example. However, he cannot make them accept the Lord. I have known of many a minister whose children were rebellious and unsaved. If children **refuse to accept Jesus into their lives, you cannot make them**.

Personally, I believe that a faithful child means **children who are respectful and obedient** to their parents. They are not unruly or rebellious but are brought up to **honor their father and mother**. Salvation is a personal experience between you and God.

Webster's New World College Dictionary defines *faithful*:

1. keeping faith; maintaining allegiance; constant; loyal: *faithful* friends
2. marked by or showing a strong sense of duty or responsibility; conscientious: *faithful* attendance

3. accurate; reliable; exact: a *faithful* copy

Children brought up in the right way (as God dictates), can be **faithful to their parents**, yet **not be a born-again believer**. If every minister and elder's child living at home had to be saved, then there would be a lot fewer ministers and elders today.

Let us also not forget about the **prophet of God, Hosea**. Hosea was told by God to go and take unto himself a wife of whoredoms and children of whoredoms. Thus, Hosea took to wife the harlot Gomer. Gomer conceived and brought forth a son, then a daughter and another son. Just because she had been a harlot before their marriage, then left him and went back to being a harlot during their marriage, does not mean that God no longer accepted Hosea as a prophet. **Hosea could not make Gomer do what was right. Neither can we make our children serve the Lord.**

Verse seven talks about the bishop and his qualifications. A bishop must be **blameless as the steward of God**. To hold the position of a bishop, a man must have **a good reputation**. His life must be blameless. He must be **surrendered to God's will** for his life. To be self-willed is to be rebellious against God. He must be able to **hold his anger in check**, not lashing out at those around him and **not given to wine**. A minister must be sober, for wine loosens the tongue of those who drink it. It also causes men to be riotous when drunk. For this cause, God says that **no drunkard will ever enter into heaven**.

1 Corinthians 5:11

But now I have written unto you not to keep company, if any man that is called a brother be a fornicator, or covetous, or an idolater, or a railer, or a drunkard, or an extortioner; with such an one no not to eat.

1 Corinthians 6:9-10

9 Know ye not that the unrighteous shall not inherit the kingdom of God? Be not deceived: neither fornicators, nor idolaters, nor adulterers, nor effeminate, nor abusers of themselves with mankind, 10 Nor thieves, nor covetous, nor drunkards, nor revilers, nor extortioners, shall inherit the kingdom of God.

Galatians 5:19-21

19 Now the works of the flesh are manifest, which are these; Adultery, fornication, uncleanness, lasciviousness,
20 Idolatry, witchcraft, hatred, variance, emulations, wrath, strife, seditions, heresies,
21 Envyings, murders, drunkenness, revellings, and such like: of the which I tell you before, as I have also told you in time past, that they which do such things shall not inherit the kingdom of God.

Furthermore, a bishop **must not be prone to fighting**, but be peaceable with all men. It goes on to say that he must **not be a lover of filthy lucre or money**. Today, as bad as I hate to say it, there are many in the ministry not because God called them, but because they are looking for an easy way to make a living. They want easy living and a good salary. If you look around, many of the mega-church pastors make millions of dollars in salary each year. Far too many pastors and ministers are making merchandise of God's people.

Reading further into verse eight, we see that a bishop must be a **lover of hospitality**. He must be one who is willing to **open his home to strangers and to meet people's needs** as best as he can. He must be friendly toward those around him, demonstrate a **genuine love for his fellow man** and have a **compassionate heart to fill the needs** of those around him.

A bishop **must be sober**, and this has nothing to do with drinking. Let us look at the word *sober*.

Merriam Webster Dictionary defines sober as:

> Marked by sedate or gravely or earnestly thoughtful character or demeanor; showing no excessive or extreme qualities of fancy, emotion or prejudice.

Now let us look at the word *just*. We can say that a man who is just is one who **deals with everyone the same**

in a fair manner and is not a cheat, liar or underhanded. He is a man of strict integrity who **lives by the principles he teaches**.

The next word we want to look at is *holy*. The scriptures teach us that **we are to be holy as God is holy**.

1 Peter 1:13-16

> [13] *Wherefore gird up the loins of your mind, be sober, and hope to the end for the grace that is to be brought unto you at the revelation of Jesus Christ;*
> [14] *As obedient children, not fashioning yourselves according to the former lusts in your ignorance:*
> [15] *But as he which hath called you is holy, so be ye holy in all manner of conversation;*
> [16] *Because it is written, Be ye holy; for I am holy.*

Being holy is to **live according to the principles** of God's Word. We at one time were sinners; however, after receiving Jesus as our personal Saviour, we are no longer sinners. The **shed blood of Jesus Christ has washed away** our sins. The old man of sin that we used to be is dead and we have become **a new creature, a new man** in Christ Jesus.

2 Corinthians 5:17

> *Therefore if any man be in Christ, he is a new creature: old things are passed away; behold, all*

things are become new.

2 Corinthians 6:9-10

[9] As unknown, and yet well known; as dying, and, behold, we live; as chastened, and not killed;
[10] As sorrowful, yet alway rejoicing; as poor, yet making many rich; as having nothing, and yet possessing all things.

Galatians 5:19-21

[19] Now the works of the flesh are manifest, which are these; Adultery, fornication, uncleanness, lasciviousness,
[20] Idolatry, witchcraft, hatred, variance, emulations, wrath, strife, seditions, heresies,
[21] Envyings, murders, drunkenness, revellings, and such like: of the which I tell you before, as I have also told you in time past, that they which do such things shall not inherit the kingdom of God.

We must strive to be the image of our Saviour and God and to **show the world that serving God makes our lives better**. As the old chorus goes:

To be like Jesus,
To be like Jesus,
All I ask is to be like Him.

All through life's journey,
From earth to glory,
All I ask is to be like Him.

The last word that we are looking at is *temperate*. To be temperate means to **be in control of yourself**, your desires, of whatever you are doing. The list depends upon your actions and desires. We must discipline our lives to **put forth a Christ-like example** for the world to see. The devil wants us to be ruled by our emotions. However, God's desire is for us, through His power, to **be in control of our emotions and desires**.

In verse nine, we read that as Christians we must **hold fast to the Word of God**. This is taught in the scriptures. We must exhort, encourage, and convince sinners by sound doctrine to **accept Jesus Christ as their personal Saviour** and Redeemer. The big question is this: Are we where God wants us to be to carry out His work?

Titus 1:10-12

[10] *For there are many unruly and vain talkers and deceivers, specially they of the circumcision:*
[11] *Whose mouths must be stopped, who subvert whole houses, teaching things which they ought not, for filthy lucre's sake.*
[12] *One of themselves, even a prophet of their own, said, The Cretians are alway liars, evil beasts, slow bellies.*

In verse ten, Paul begins to talk about a certain group of people who were unruly. They talked continually saying vain and untrue things. Satan used this group to deceive their fellow man. Paul goes on to say of this group that a large portion of them were of the circumcision.

These Jews were set on destroying the Christian church. Unruly means that **they were rebellious against authority of any kind**. They continually spoke blasphemy, deceit, and lying, and worked discord anywhere possible. They did not care **what damage or trouble they caused**. Rather, they took great pleasure in others' distress.

One example is that they were teaching the early church members that to be saved they must be circumcised. These men believed in their traditions more than in the saving power of Jesus Christ. Sadly, they did much damage to the early church, leading many astray from the truth of God's Word. What we, as Christians, should be very much aware of is that **the lies of evil men and women are believed most of the time over the truth**.

Titus 1:11

Whose mouths must be stopped, who subvert whole houses, teaching things which they ought not, for filthy lucre's sake.

Paul, in verse eleven, says of these men that their mouths are to be stopped and that **their lies are be countered by the truth of the gospel**. He continues by telling us that these purveyors of evil subvert whole houses with their lies, leading men and women from the liberty of Christ into the bondage of the traditions of men for their own profits.

Titus 1:12

One of themselves, even a prophet of their own,
said, The Cretians are alway liars, evil beasts, slow
bellies.

Paul continues in twelve by **telling us what the Cretians** (or Cretans in modern language) **were really like**. Today, we look around us at the world and we see that certain people – even countries – are known for certain characteristics. For example, the Egyptians were known for their great buildings, the Philistines for their brutality and the Cretians were known for their demoralizing lifestyle. They were carnal and extremely worldly. It has been said that they were all liars. They were not merely beasts, they were evil beasts. Paul finishes by describing them as lazy and gluttonous.

To understand more of why Paul speaks the way he does, we need to **look at the background of the people of Crete and where they came from**. The island was settled by people from Asia Minor who were known as the Minoans because of their King. According to legend, King Minos was the son of the god Zeus and the goddess Europa. Myths of him state that he was a lawmaker and ruler of the great Minoan Empire, a very cruel conqueror and a hard taskmaster. Greek legends state that King Minos demanded of Athens seven boys and seven girls each year for sacrifice to the Minotaur. All that remains of the great Minoan civilization today is ruins of their great buildings and art after the armies of Rome conquered the Minoans in the year 68 B.C.

The Cretians were, by the time of Paul, considered to be the lowest of the low, known everywhere for their lying, their cruelty to one another and their lewd behavior as drunkards who were gluttonous, self-willed and unruly, **a people who very much needed God**.

For this reason, Paul told Titus to rebuke them sharply. This goes against what most people believe that a Christian should be in today's world. I will repeat this again and again, **we must not let the world dictate what we are to believe and how we should act**. The world tells us that Christians are to be meek and mild like Jesus was. However, they do not read their Bibles. Jesus got **angry at times with how people tried to use God for their own purposes**. As we look at scripture, we see how Jesus became angry.

Mark 3:5

> *And when he had looked round about on them with anger, being grieved for the hardness of their hearts, he saith unto the man, Stretch forth thine hand. And he stretched it out: and his hand was*

restored whole as the other.

Mark 11:15-19

¹⁵ And they come to Jerusalem: and Jesus went into the temple, and began to cast out them that sold and bought in the temple, and overthrew the tables of the moneychangers, and the seats of them that sold doves;

¹⁶ And would not suffer that any man should carry any vessel through the temple.

¹⁷ And he taught, saying unto them, Is it not written, My house shall be called of all nations the house of prayer? but ye have made it a den of thieves.

¹⁸ And the scribes and chief priests heard it, and sought how they might destroy him: for they feared him, because all the people was astonished at his doctrine.

¹⁹ And when even was come, he went out of the city.

Luke 19:45-47

⁴⁵ And he went into the temple, and began to cast out them that sold therein, and them that bought;

⁴⁶ Saying unto them, It is written, My house is the house of prayer: but ye have made it a den of thieves.

⁴⁷ And he taught daily in the temple. But the chief priests and the scribes and the chief of the people

sought to destroy him,

John 2:13-16

¹³ And the Jews' passover was at hand, and Jesus went up to Jerusalem,
¹⁴ And found in the temple those that sold oxen and sheep and doves, and the changers of money sitting:
¹⁵ And when he had made a scourge of small cords, he drove them all out of the temple, and the sheep, and the oxen; and poured out the changers' money, and overthrew the tables;
¹⁶ And said unto them that sold doves, Take these things hence; make not my Father's house an house of merchandise.

There are times when **we all become angry**; it is just part of being human. The thing is that we are **not to let our anger control us**. We are to control our anger. The man and woman who **control their anger preserve their relationship with Jesus Christ** and win the victory over sin.

Ephesians 4:26-27

²⁶ Be ye angry, and sin not: let not the sun go down upon your wrath:
²⁷ Neither give place to the devil.

In *The John Phillips Commentary Series,* we read:

> The concept of a mild Jesus is entirely false. Scripture reveals that He knew anger (Mark 3:5) and that He took a whip and drove the money changers from the temple (John 2:13-17). He denounced the religious Jewish leaders of His day as hypocrites, children of hell, fools, and a "generation of vipers" (Matt. 12:34), and He said that they were blind, unclean, and full of iniquity. He knew full well that the religious establishment was conspiring to put Him to death, but He continued to be fearless in His denunciations.

We, as Christians, must **stand up for what is right according to the Word of God**. Peter, Paul and Titus proclaimed the Word of God and so must all of us today. **All of the saved, born-again believers must do the same.** We must **warn the lost inside and outside** of the churches. God's eternal judgement is coming upon the lost souls who refuse to take a stand for what is right. We cannot help sinners by sinking down to their level. We must **lift them up to a better life** in Christ Jesus. We must make them acquainted with Jesus and His saving power. If we love the lost, then we will **tell them about Jesus and His saving grace**.

Titus 1:13-16

¹³ This witness is true. Wherefore rebuke them sharply, that they may be sound in the faith;
¹⁴ Not giving heed to Jewish fables, and commandments of men, that turn from the truth.
¹⁵ Unto the pure all things are pure: but unto them that are defiled and unbelieving is nothing pure; but even their mind and conscience is defiled.
¹⁶ They profess that they know God; but in works they deny him, being abominable, and disobedient, and unto every good work reprobate.

In verse thirteen, Paul was neither careful nor gentle in his remarks concerning the people of Crete, for he was well aware of their ways before writing to Titus. Paul was affirming to Titus that all that Titus had heard about the Cretians was most assuredly true. It was very important that Titus be **continually on guard in dealing with the people** of Crete.

Paul in this verse tells Titus to rebuke the Cretians, and to rebuke them sharply in the matter of serving the Lord. **There could be no error in serving the Lord.** Titus was not to let anyone get by with **changing or subverting the truth** of the gospel message.

People always feel better when the gospel message is diluted down so that they can do the things they want to do. If we want to be effective in leading souls to the Lord, **we must be truthful in everything that we say and do.**

There are too many already that hold to the doctrine of "Do as I say and not as I do."

There are far too many blind leaders of the blind in our midst today. We must **learn to serve God and to do His will**, not the will of the self-serving people around us. Paul was concerned about the saints of God. We must be **sound in the doctrine of Jesus Christ**, for there are many unscrupulous people who are out to make merchandise of God's people. We must know the truth, for **the truth is the only thing that sets us free** from all sin and bondage.

John 8:32, 36

> *32 And ye shall know the truth, and the truth shall make you free.*
> *36 If the Son therefore shall make you free, ye shall be free indeed.*

Galatians 5:1

> *Stand fast therefore in the liberty wherewith Christ hath made us free, and be not entangled again with the yoke of bondage.*

One of the tricks of the devil then and now is to bring in men to pervert the gospel, to bring into the church fables and the commandments of men in an attempt to turn the saints away from the truth of the gospel of Jesus Christ. We must, as I have said so many times, **always be on**

guard against the tricks of the enemy of our souls.

Here is a perfect example of what I am talking about. I knew a minister that would always quote this scripture: "Ye know not what manner of spirit ye are." I knew this did not sound right, because I knew if I was saved or not. Therefore, I looked the scripture up and found out that this minister left off one word, the word "of." It changed the whole meaning of the scripture. Luke 9:55 states, . . . *"Ye know not what manner of spirit ye are of."* This **changing of scriptures is happening every day**.

We must be on the **lookout for the deceptions and devices of Satan**. Some modern Bibles do not call Mary, the mother of Jesus, a virgin; they say she was a young maid. In doing this, they are doing away with the virgin birth of Jesus Christ. They are saying that Jesus is not the Son of God, that in fact Jesus was an illegitimate child. The lies of Satan are abounding in the churches today.

I remember in the fourth grade the teacher telling the class that the story of Jonah and the whale was a lie. A whale did not swallow Jonah, since a whale could not swallow anything as big as golf balls. However, **Jesus called the great fish a whale** in Matthew 12:40, and I will **believe what Jesus has said over anything that man** might say.

Just as in Paul's day, we have among us those who desire to destroy the true gospel of Jesus Christ. They tell people that they love them and care about them. However, at the same time, they refuse to preach against sin and its result to the soul. Where do they show this love when they refuse to warn people about the results of their sins?

When I was growing up, my parents would spank me when I did something that I knew was wrong. They would **tell me that they spanked me because they loved me** and wanted me to grow up knowing right from wrong. At the time, I felt that if they truly loved me then they would not have spanked me. However, as I grew up, I began to see that **loving someone means you do what is best for him or her** if you truly care. God is our heavenly Father and at times **we will receive a "spanking" from Him when we are wrong because He truly loves us**.

In these last days, we are seeing more and more of what Paul was warning Titus about. The devil is trying every trick in his book to diminish the power of the gospel. When the Bible **tells us that something is sin, then it is sin, no matter how some try to explain** it away. The Ten Commandments are still the Ten Commandments, even though many are trying to tell us that they are only ten suggestions as to how we should live. I, like you, do not like to be told that I am wrong. However, **if I am wrong, then I am wrong**.

Once again, there is a trend in today's churches to try and bring back Jewish traditions. The very thing that Titus was fighting in Crete is rising up again. Some Christian churches are observing Jewish high holy days and Jewish feast days. These things were **done away with when Jesus died** upon the Cross of Calvary. They are part of the past; they are not a part of Christianity. We are no longer under the Old Testament. We are **part of the New**

Testament, **the church of Jesus Christ** the Redeemer.

Jesus came to fulfill the law, to institute **a new covenant between man and God**. The Bible teaches us that if we follow the law, then we are bound by the law, and grace is of none effect. The church world needs to **decide if they will live under grace or be bound** by the law.

Titus 1:15

Unto the pure all things are pure: but unto them that are defiled and unbelieving is nothing pure; but even their mind and conscience is defiled.

As we begin to look at verse fifteen, we find that the **first half of this verse has a twofold meaning**. *"Unto the pure all things are pure."* The first meaning we look at is food. To be **pure in Christ means that there are no foods that are impure** and that cannot be eaten. We are not under the Jewish dietary laws.

The second meaning deals with our **spiritual condition and lives**. When we meet Jesus Christ and accept Him as our Saviour, Jesus comes into our hearts to live. This inner power of Jesus Christ that resides in us **gives us the power to refuse sin and walk in the newness of Jesus Christ** and to refuse to allow sin to have dominion in our lives.

However, to the sinner, the unbelieving, there is

nothing pure since their very minds and thoughts are continually evil and sinful. Sadly, **the sinner cannot change on his or her own**. They may change a few things they are doing; nevertheless, their sin is still there. Try as they might, **they cannot cleanse themselves from sin**. Their only hope is in Jesus Christ, since **Jesus is the only one who can forgive sin** and wash it away.

Nearly forty years ago, my wife and I went to visit a woman we had met in church. She told us of a church that she had attended, and in this church, they had some **very peculiar beliefs**. They believed that a person could be saved, becoming a born-again believer, and be possessed of demons at the same time. **They tried to teach her how to stand in front of a mirror and cast demons out of herself**. To many a person, this seems like a funny story. However, it is not. People are teaching these very ideas and practices to men and women today.

The devil is unscrupulous and will try any trick that he can to lead people astray. However, this is not any more outrageous than that a person can be a Christian and still sin every day. **If it is a sin before you are saved, then it is still sin after you are saved.** Sin will send us to a devil's hell.

There are so many today who profess to know God; however, **their lives do not bear record to their profession**. As scripture states, there are many who have a form of Godliness but **deny the power thereof** and from such, **turn away**.

38

2 Timothy 3:5

Having a form of godliness, but denying the power thereof: from such turn away.

Titus 1:16

They profess that they know God; but in works they deny him, being abominable, and disobedient, and unto every good work reprobate.

The last part of verse sixteen states: "*but in works they deny Him, being abominable, and disobedient, and unto every good work reprobate.*" There are multitudes who **say that they believe in God**. However, they do not live for Him nor claim to. **How can a person truly say that they believe in God and not serve Him?** They are disobedient to God by their actions, doing those things which are against God's will.

Chapter One - Review Questions

1. To whom are the promises of God given?

_____

_____

_____

2. Which book of the Bible tells us that for everything there is a season?

_____

_____

_____

3. What is the common faith?

_____

_____

_____

4. Why was Titus left on the island of Crete?

_____

_____

_____

5. What does "setting a church in order" mean?

_____

_____

_____

6. What does it mean to be holy as God is holy?

_____

_____

7. The devil wants us to be ruled by our emotions, however God's desire is for us to . . .

_____

_____

_____

8. Where did the people of Crete originally come from?

_____

_____

9. How was Titus to rebuke the Cretians?

_____

_____

Chapter 2

Titus 2:1

But speak thou the things which become sound doctrine:

In verse one, Paul is giving Titus **more instructions concerning the Cretian church**. First and by far the most important thing to do was to **establish the Cretians in sound doctrine**. False teachers were bombarding the Cretian churches with their false doctrines. They were individuals that the Bible describes as blind leaders of the blind and having a form of godliness but denying the true power thereof. The Bible instructs us to turn away from such as these.

2 Timothy 3:1-5

> [1] *This know also, that in the last days perilous times shall come.*
> [2] *For men shall be lovers of their own selves,*

43

covetous, boasters, proud, blasphemers, disobedient to parents, unthankful, unholy,

[3] Without natural affection, trucebreakers, false accusers, incontinent, fierce, despisers of those that are good,

[4] Traitors, heady, highminded, lovers of pleasures more than lovers of God;

[5] Having a form of godliness, but denying the power thereof: from such turn away.

The church of today, like the Cretian churches, is **constantly under attack from all sides**. The sooner that people realize that the **truth of God's Word is the only thing that can truly set us free**, the better their lives will become.

Psalm 127:1

Except the LORD build the house, they labour in vain that build it: except the LORD keep the city, the watchman waketh but in vain.

Except God build the house, they that labor, labor in vain. The **Word of God is the only foundation that the church** can stand upon; when we build our lives upon the truth of the scriptures, we are **building a spiritual house that will stand the test of time**. Fads and fashions will come and go; however, God's Word was established **and is forevermore established in heaven and in the earth**. The

44

false doctrines that are put forth today may sound good to the flesh; nevertheless, in the end they all lead to spiritual death. Saints, we must **crucify our fleshly desires and let the Lord reign** in our hearts and lives.

I realize this is hard to do in today's world. The **Word of God is our foundation**, the foundation upon which we **build our spiritual lives**. That foundation is being eroded every day. Church denominations that built their churches on the divine scriptures are today taking their spiritual foundations and tearing them apart. They are changing **their tenets of faith to please the demands** of Satan's crowd.

Abortion, the murder of innocent babies is no longer a sin. Life is no longer sacred.

Currently, on the homosexual front in America, it is no longer a sin to practice homosexuality. Also, in most states, homosexual marriages are now allowed. The world looks on the homosexual lifestyle as "normal" and does not see it as sinning.

However, **it is in God's eyes, and this they cannot change**.

This year, the governor of California signed a bill giving judges the right to decide if someone no more than ten years older than a minor can have sex (of any form) with said minor and not have to be listed as a sexual offender. This is taking an additional step toward making pedophilia legal.

The fleshly desires of sinners are reaching new heights of depravity. Every day, the ungodly push more and more to undermine God's church. Our **spiritual foundation and our Christian beliefs are being put to the test** to see if we will stand for God. May God have mercy upon His church and **send Jesus to take us home**.

Titus 2:2

That the aged men be sober, grave, temperate,
sound in faith, in charity, in patience.

In this second verse, Paul gives Titus instructions concerning the **aged or older men in the churches**. The older people are generally **the foundation of the church**. Titus was to be sure that the aged men in the churches were **good examples of what a Christian should be**. They were to be sober. Most modern commentators say that the word sober means a person who does not drink alcohol. In *Barnes' Notes on the New Testament*, Barnes states that **the word sober means vigilant**. A man who is vigilant will **not be found doing the will of the devil**.

In *Barnes' Notes on the New Testament*, Rev. Barnes gives this definition:

> *Sober.* σωφρονα. Properly, a man of a
> sound mind; one who follows sound reason,
> and who is not under the control of passion.
> The idea is that he should have his desires
> and passions well regulated. Perhaps the

46

word prudent would come nearer to the meaning of the apostle than any single word which we have.

Another thing that Titus was to watch for in the aged men was **that they should be grave**. The word grave means serious. To be serious minded does not mean that a person cannot enjoy life. The aged man, by living a long life, has gained much **wisdom that can be very useful** to others. Never underestimate the wisdom of the aged. The common idea that the aged men of the world are good for nothing is a falsehood. They possess **a world of untapped knowledge**.

Paul is telling Timothy what an aged Christian man's life should be. He should be **temperate or self-controlled, not given to excess**, but wise in his actions as becomes a child of God. Most of all he must be **sound in the doctrine of faith** in Jesus Christ. He needs to know what he believes and **why he believes it**. He should be well versed in the gospel message and **ready to give an answer when asked**.

He must also have charity (or a spirit of love) for **those around him and for the lost souls of sinners**. One of our Lord's main directives was that we love one another. Without a Christ-like love, our lives are lacking. Love will attract those around us and **give us a chance to spread the good news** of Jesus Christ and what He has done for us.

Along with a Christian love, it is essential that we **have patience with the world around us**. We must wait before God, **not moving rashly**. There is an old saying that says fools rush in where angels fear to tread. Many times, reacting rashly causes failure and turns people away from God. Patience is a virtue that **every Christian must learn** to have in their lives.

Titus 2:3-5

³ The aged women likewise, that they be in behaviour as becometh holiness, not false accusers, not given to much wine, teachers of good things; ⁴ That they may teach the young women to be sober, to love their husbands, to love their children, ⁵ To be discreet, chaste, keepers at home, good, obedient to their own husbands, that the word of God be not blasphemed.

In these three verses, Paul carries on his instructions to Timothy. Here Paul is talking about how **aged or older women in the church should conduct themselves** as becomes holiness. The aged Christian women were to **be of good behavior**. They were to be a **living witness of what holiness should be** in the lives of Godly women.

Paul uses the word likewise when he begins to talk about the women of older years. These women were to be **in good behavior before the younger women** in the church. Paul states that they were **to live a life of example**, or a life that becomes holiness. Their walk in life was to **promote a life surrendered to God**. They were not to be talebearers or false accusers. Gossiping is one of the surest ways to spread discord among the members of the churches. It matters not whether it is done by a woman or a man, gossip can kill a person's witness before the church and the world. Gossiping is the same as being a false accuser. For almost all gossip is falsehoods told by idle people who have nothing else to do. The scriptures tell us that **we are not to be a gossip**.

Proverbs 11:13

> *A talebearer revealeth secrets: but he that is of a faithful spirit concealeth the matter.*

Proverbs 18:8

> *The words of a talebearer are as wounds, and they go down into the innermost parts of the belly.*

Proverbs 20:19

> *He that goeth about as a talebearer revealeth secrets: therefore meddle not with him that flattereth with his lips.*

The aged women were **not to be given to much wine**, for wine loosens the tongue and a person's inhibitions to the point that they will do and say things that should not be done or said. Scripture tells us woe unto him that gives his neighbor drink. Strong drink is a tool used by Satan to destroy people's lives, especially those who profess to being Christians. There are numerous scriptures that tell us that **no drunkard will ever enter into heaven**.

Habakkuk 2:15

> *Woe unto him that giveth his neighbour drink, that puttest thy bottle to him, and makest him drunken also, that thou mayest look on their nakedness!*

1 Corinthians 6:9-10

> *[9] Know ye not that the unrighteous shall not inherit the kingdom of God? Be not deceived: neither fornicators, nor idolaters, nor adulterers, nor effeminate, nor abusers of themselves with mankind, [10] Nor thieves, nor covetous, nor drunkards, nor revilers, nor extortioners, shall inherit the kingdom of God.*

Galatians 5:19-21

> *[19] Now the works of the flesh are manifest, which are these; Adultery, fornication, uncleanness, lasciviousness,*
> *[20] Idolatry, witchcraft, hatred, variance, emulations, wrath, strife, seditions, heresies,*
> *[21] Envyings, murders, drunkenness, revellings, and*

such like: of the which I tell you before, as I have also told you in time past, that they which do such things shall not inherit the kingdom of God.

In looking at these scriptures, they point to the **absolute forbidding of the use of alcohol to Christian believers** everywhere.

The last portion of this third verse tells us that the aged women in the churches were to be **teachers of the good things of God**. The aged women and men were to be **examples of the goodness of God and of what God will do for those** who love Him and serve Him.

Titus 2:4

That they may teach the young women to be sober, to love their husbands, to love their children,

As we begin to look at the first of this scripture, it tells us what the older women of the church were to do in the churches. Paul calls these older women **to teach and be an example** to the younger women. The younger women were to be **sober and not given to the use of wine**. They were also to **teach the younger women to love and care** for their husbands. You might ask why wives needed to be taught to love their husbands. Just remember that things were a lot different in those days.

In most of the world today, men and women meet each other, date, and fall in love. Then they get married.

This is the way that it is supposed to be. In other cases, couples do not marry. They decide to just live together for a while. Sometimes they live together for years and even have children together, even though this is against God's will. It is almost as if they take pleasure in disobeying the will of God.

In the days of the early church, this was not the way marriage worked. Marriages were **arranged by the parents of the young people**. In most of those arranged marriages, the bride had **little to no say about the man** she was to marry. In some of these arranged marriages, even the bridegroom had no say about the woman he was to marry.

Today, many countries still practice arranged marriages. These young women do not love their husbands and **sometimes do not even know them**. Such was the case in Titus' time. Often, the young women had never even seen the men they were marrying. She **met her husband for the first time** during the wedding ceremony.

The older Christian women were to **teach and instruct these younger women how to begin to love** their husbands. They were to teach them about the problems that they were facing and going to face. Many of the young wives were spending their wedding night with a complete stranger. Their life was not easy; it would be a lot easier for them if they **learned to love their husbands**. Furthermore, they were to **help these women to love their children** regardless of who their husband was and how they felt about him.

Many times, we think that we have it hard. Maybe we need to **take time to think of how life was in the early church world**.

Titus 2:5

To be discreet, chaste, keepers at home, good, obedient to their own husbands, that the word of God be not blasphemed.

All women whether young or old **were to be discreet**. Many women and men in today's world do not look at things the way scriptures tell us to. The young people today need teaching in **what is right and what is wrong in the light of God's Word**. Acting in the wrong way will bring reproach upon them, the church, and the message they give out. **We all need to be self-disciplined**. Paul is talking about how women need to be in self-control in the way that they conduct themselves. They can be an **asset to their husbands and their fellow Christians**, or they can be a detriment to them. Self-control (self-discipline) is something every Christian needs in order to **show a Christ-like example to those whom we meet**. A Christian woman is to be chaste, to be **pure in her heart and mind**.

Webster's New World College Dictionary defines *chaste* as:

1. not indulging in unlawful sexual activity; virtuous

2. sexually abstinent; celibate
3. pure, decent, or modest in nature, behavior, etc.
4. restrained and simple in style; not ornate

A Christian woman who is chaste in her mind and most of all her heart **will be true to her Lord and Saviour**, Jesus Christ, as well as **to her husband and family**. She will bring **honor to her husband**, and those who know him will praise him.

The older women were to teach the younger women **the importance of being good homemakers**, of tending to the affairs of the home. In today's world, the trend is for women to work outside of the home. Many of today's marriages fall apart because of discontent when both partners must work. The family unit is strained when mothers must work and leave their children with others. **The children suffer when both parents must work.** It is also **hard on the parents** trying to make ends meet in addition to giving the children quality time. Their lives become so busy that they **hardly have time for each other**. They are so busy that support from other family members and friends begins to fade away. They begin to feel that no one cares about them anymore. They feel as though **they are on their own without anyone**.

When our lives get so busy that we do not have time to visit or receive visitors, then **we are too busy for our own good**. When we cut ourselves off from those who care about us, we hurt them, and more importantly, we are **hurting ourselves the most**. In today's world, the family tends to split, and each member goes their own separate way. This is not good. We must **take the time to be a family**. We must have the **time to bond together**, to be a well-connected family unit. If you say that you cannot find the time to do this, then **you must make the time**, even if you must let something else go. Just as important, if not more so, is that we must **make time for God**, our **family**, and then the **church**, in that order.

As we continue to look at this verse, we begin to see that Paul **realized the importance of the older Christian women**. Paul states that the older women were to teach the younger to be good. Being good means being kind, gentle, and good to others as well as having an attitude of hospitality.

"Obedient to their own husband." Here, we see a problem **also prevalent in today's world**. In the days of the early church (and for hundreds of years afterward) women were obedient to their husbands. Today, the world has drastically changed. The women's equal rights movement has caused women to demand independence from men, to insist on equality to their husbands to the point of ruling over them, often with disastrous results. Being obedient (cooperative) to them is no longer in their idea of marriage. This is just another way that the devil is trying to destroy the home and family.

Satan knows that the home and the family are a major part of God's plan for people's lives and that the husband is to be the head of the household. There can **only be one head**. Anything with two heads is a freak.

Therefore, the **wife is to be obedient** to her husband. The husband is **not to be cruel to his wife**. He is to be loving and caring and kind, as **this is also God's plan**. We find that the scriptures tell us that **husbands are to love their wives**.

Colossians 3:19

> *Husbands, love your wives, and be not bitter against them.*

Ephesians 5:25

> *Husbands, love your wives, even as Christ also loved the church, and gave himself for it;*

The wife is to be her **husband's helper, his support, and obedient in all decisions** they make together. The wife is to be **part of the decision-making**, then she is to be **obedient to all the decisions** they make. To be disobedient to her husband is to blaspheme the Word of God by being disobedient to God's Word. God's plan for the family is **plainly stated in the scriptures**. All we must do is to **search the scriptures to find God's plan**.

Titus 2:6-8

> *[6] Young men likewise exhort to be sober minded.*
> *[7] In all things shewing thyself a pattern of good*

works: in doctrine shewing uncorruptness, gravity, sincerity,
[8] Sound speech, that cannot be condemned; that he that is of the contrary part may be ashamed, having no evil thing to say of you.

This sixth verse addresses young men. These young men were **to be sober minded**. Again, sober minded means to be serious minded, to **gain control over their youthful lusts** and desires. As with all young men, these young men were easily distracted by the things going on around them. This is an ongoing thing with all young men the world around.

In verse seven, Paul was telling Titus to **be an example to the young men** in the churches. Titus was to **show in his own life a pattern of good works** by putting forth a Christ-like example before the people in the churches and living an **uncorrupted life with gravity or sedateness of manner** and sincerity.

Paul was a **man on a mission for Jesus** Christ. Before his salvation, Paul had a zeal to stamp out the Christian movement, yet when he met Jesus on the road to Damascus, Jesus **turned that zeal into a zeal to spread the gospel message** to the Gentiles. This calling was so strong that **Paul had very little time for levity**. The preaching and teaching of God's Word were serious business, for there were souls to be saved. Paul expected Titus to be just as serious as he was. The plan of salvation, **Jesus sacrificed on the cross for lost souls**, must be their main work.

The young men in the churches were to show a **sense of sincerity**, a deep **trust in the love and power** of God. They must be **proven examples of what the Lord does at salvation**, knowing that all was well with their souls before God. They were to have a **deep abiding peace within**, a peace that **the world did not give and the world could not take away**.

In verse eight, Paul finishes his instructions to Titus by saying to him to use *"sound speech, that cannot be condemned."* In so doing, all those who condemned God's servants might find themselves ashamed and then **have no more to say against the Christians**. We all must be of sound speech and doctrine before this lost world. We are to be **particularly careful not to do or say anything that can bring reproach** upon God's Word. We must be sure to **base everything we say upon the Word of God**. Remember, the Word of God is the **only absolute authority for Christian believers** to stand on.

Titus 2:9-10

[9] Exhort servants to be obedient unto their own masters, and to please them well in all things; not answering again;
[10] Not purloining, but shewing all good fidelity; that they may adorn the doctrine of God our Saviour in all things.

In these two verses, Paul addresses the issue of **servants and slaves and how they were to conduct** themselves after they became born-again believers. Paul tells these individuals that they are to be **obedient to their masters**. These servants were to **do their masters' bidding, whatever tasks they were told to do**. They were to please their masters and to **do it gladly, not grudgingly**, realizing that the Lord is their true spiritual master, and **pleasing the Lord means pleasing their earthly masters**. The only exception to this rule would be when their masters told them to do things that were against God's Holy Word.

The servants and slaves were **not to backtalk their masters**. Paul states it this way, *"not answering again."* One of the surest ways to incur their masters' wrath was to backtalk them. To grumble, gripe and complain is not giving a Christ-like example to their masters or to those watching their lives looking to find mistakes and faults.

Today, for those of us who work outside the home, we are to have a **similar attitude toward our bosses** as the servants and slaves of Paul's day were expected to display toward their masters. We hire ourselves out to work for a day's pay. We are to be **the best workers possible, showing a Christ-like example** to those around us.

In verse ten, we read that a **servant should not be purloining**. What this means is that the servants were not to steal from their masters. In Paul's day, it was very common for slaves and servants to take small objects from their master's homes and sell them. This usually was the only way that they could get any money for themselves. Life for servants and slaves was very hard most of the time.

Today, we may no longer be slaves, but the same rules apply to us. We, as Christians, must **show love and honor to everyone**. We must be an **example of right living and conduct**. We must be very careful in everything, for the world is watching for us to fail. We must **not take small objects from our jobs**. The taking of small things like pens or paperclips without permission is stealing. Stealing of anything is **still a sin in the eyes of God**.

We are to **show a Christ-like spirit to everyone** on and off our jobs. We are to live in such a manner that God is glorified by our very lives. We are to be **honest and trustworthy before all men**, for in doing so, we honor our Saviour and King, Jesus Christ.

Titus 2:11-12

[11] For the grace of God that bringeth salvation hath appeared to all men,
[12] Teaching us that, denying ungodliness and worldly lusts, we should live soberly, righteously, and godly, in this present world;

In this eleventh verse, Paul comes back to the main theme of the scriptures, the **saving grace of God through Jesus Christ our Lord**. This grace makes it possible for humanity to **have their sins forgiven**, washed away by the redeeming blood of the Lamb of God.

In the Old Testament days, the sacrificing of

animals would postpone God's judgement for another year. However, it was only from one year to the next. What the blood of animals could not do, the **redeeming blood of God's only Son**, Jesus Christ, did. This was the **supreme sacrifice, the final sacrifice**.

When we think of grace, every Christian must realize that **grace means unmerited favor**. It is not something that we deserve, nor can we earn it by our acts or deeds. Grace is a **gift to us from God, a gift that cannot do us any good until we accept it** and act upon it.

Romans 5:21

> *That as sin hath reigned unto death, even so might grace reign through righteousness unto eternal life by Jesus Christ our Lord.*

2 Corinthians 12:9

> *And he said unto me, My grace is sufficient for thee: for my strength is made perfect in weakness. Most gladly therefore will I rather glory in my infirmities, that the power of Christ may rest upon me.*

God's grace is **sufficient for all of our problems and trials** as long as we trust in Jesus and live for Him. As I sit here, that old gospel song comes to my mind, *Amazing Grace*. It carries a message that speaks to our souls. Written by John Newton, it **speaks of his experience at salvation**.

Amazing Grace

Amazing Grace, how sweet the sound,
That saved a wretch like me.
I once was lost but now am found,
Was blind, but now I see.

T'was Grace that taught my heart to fear.
And Grace, my fears relieved.
How precious did that Grace appear
The hour I first believed.

Through many dangers, toils and snares
I have already come;
'Tis Grace that brought me safe thus far
and Grace will lead me home.

The Lord has promised good to me.
His word my hope secures.
He will my shield and portion be,
As long as life endures.

Yea, when this flesh and heart shall fail,
And mortal life shall cease,
I shall possess within the veil,
A life of joy and peace.

When we've been here ten thousand years

Bright shining as the sun.
We've no less days to sing God's praise
Than when we've first begun.

The amazing grace of God **passes all understanding**. Saints, we are blessed, we are blessed. Nevertheless, many who call themselves Christians live as if they have never felt the touch of the saving grace of God. When we come to Jesus for salvation and we repent of all of our sins, **our lives are forever changed**. Grace comes into our lives, we are changed, and we are **transformed from the old creature of sin into a brand-new person** in Christ Jesus. A new **Christ-like nature replaces the old selfish man** of sin. If there is no change, then **there has been no salvation**. Today, there are many who preach that you can be saved and still live like the devil. You can still keep doing the same old worldly things. My friend, this is not so. It is a lie of the devil trying to deceive you and bring you down.

Many years ago, I worked with a man who claimed to be a Christian. One day we were talking, and I asked him this question: "Before you got saved, you got drunk, you cheated on your wife, stole things; is this right?" He answered, "Yes." I then asked him, "Today, you claim to be saved." He answered, "Yes, I am." I then asked what he was saved from, since he still did all of the same things that he did before he claimed to have gotten saved. "Well," he said, "I am saved from all of my sins." He then told me this, "After you get saved, it does not matter what you do.

You are still saved."

This man believes a lie that the devil is perpetrating. Sin is sin. **If it condemns you before you are saved, it will still condemn you after you are saved.** Salvation does not give license to go out and sin after salvation. If this were so, then God would be a respecter of persons, which he is not. **We are either saved or a sinner.** There is no such thing as a saved sinner. You are either **a sinner or a born-again child of God** who is blood-bought and redeemed.

The gift of salvation through the grace of God teaches us to **live in a godly manner in this present world**. We are to **deny ungodliness, worldliness and fleshly desires** and lust. We are to live honestly and up-rightly before this present world and to be a **living example of what God can and will do** for those who serve Him.

Who will walk upright before Him?

Barnes' Notes on the New Testament reads:

> The phrase "worldly lusts" refers to all improper desires pertaining to this life – the desire of wealth, pleasure, honour, sensual indulgence. It refers to such passions as the men of this world are prone to and would include all those things which cannot be indulged in with a proper reference to the world to come. The gross passions would be of course included, and all those more refined

pleasures also which constitute the charac-
teristic and peculiar enjoyments of those who
do not live unto God.

It seems that the world has not changed very much
down through the centuries. Paul, in ending this twelfth
verse, makes it very plain that **we are to live a life pleasing
to God**. We are to be sober – keeping ourselves **under
control**, not yielding to the desires of the flesh and
righteous – **living an upright life in the presence of God**
and the world around us. We are to be honest, **keep our
word to others**, and be kind to all men **regardless of their
status in life**. We are to be a person of good moral
scruples. All of this we are to **be now in this present**
world.

Titus 2:13-15

*¹³ Looking for that blessed hope, and the glorious
appearing of the great God and our Saviour Jesus
Christ;*
*¹⁴ Who gave himself for us, that he might redeem us
from all iniquity, and purify unto himself a peculiar
people, zealous of good works.*
*¹⁵ These things speak, and exhort, and rebuke with
all authority. Let no man despise thee.*

In this thirteenth verse, we have Paul encouraging
us to **look forward to the coming of our Lord** and

Saviour, Jesus Christ. We are to **look with an expectation** for His soon return to take us home. When we have loved ones coming to see us, we **look forward to their coming** with great anticipation. When they arrive, we are **happy to see them and rejoice**. How much more we should be looking for the **coming of Jesus to take us home to be with Him** forever, for **Jesus is our hope and future**. Without Him, there is nothing.

This reminds me of another person who **looked with anticipation while expecting to receive**. This man, being crippled from birth, was **carried every day to the gate of the temple** to beg for his living. One day, he saw Peter and John coming to the temple. As they came close, he began to ask alms of them. He hoped, perhaps even **expected to receive money from them**. However, he received **a lot more than he dreamed of**. Peter and John told him that they had no money, but in the name of Jesus to **rise up and walk**. When he accepted what they offered, **he immediately received his healing with great joy**. He went into the temple **walking and leaping and praising God**.

Acts 3:1-8

> *[1] Now Peter and John went up together into the temple at the hour of prayer, being the ninth hour.*
> *[2] And a certain man lame from his mother's womb was carried, whom they laid daily at the gate of the temple which is called Beautiful, to ask alms of*

them that entered into the temple;

³ Who seeing Peter and John about to go into the temple asked an alms.

⁴ And Peter, fastening his eyes upon him with John, said, Look on us.

⁵ And he gave heed unto them, expecting to receive something of them.

⁶ Then Peter said, Silver and gold have I none; but such as I have give I thee: In the name of Jesus Christ of Nazareth rise up and walk.

⁷ And he took him by the right hand, and lifted him up: and immediately his feet and ankle bones received strength.

⁸ And he leaping up stood, and walked, and entered with them into the temple, walking, and leaping, and praising God.

When we pray, we **need to expect God to hear us** and to answer. For **when we expect to receive**, we shall receive, because we **have put our faith into action**. Paul is telling us to **look with expectation for our blessed hope**, the coming of our Redeemer and Saviour, Jesus Christ. His coming is **even at the door**. My friend, if **you are not looking for Jesus to return**, I can assure you that you will not see Him when He comes.

Hebrews 9:28

So Christ was once offered to bear the sins of many;

and unto them that look for him shall he appear the second time without sin unto salvation.

It is time for all of God's saints to lift up their heads, for **our redemption draws nigh**. Paul reminds Titus and each of us of **the price that was paid for our salvation** and of how **Jesus gave Himself for all of us to redeem us** back unto God.

We can **once again come into fellowship with God**. We **no longer need to take a sacrifice to a priest** to be offered for our sins. When Jesus died upon the cross, the veil in the temple **was rent into two pieces** from the top to the bottom. This signified that **no longer was man separated** from God. We no longer need to go to a priest, for **now we have access to God directly** in prayer.

To all who repent and trust in God, He **purifies us to Himself**. He makes us a peculiar people, a people who **do good works in the name** of Jesus Christ. Through salvation, Jesus **changes our lives**. The old sinful nature dies, and a **new nature or man** comes into being. We become a person **who loves truth and honesty and takes great joy in telling the world about what Jesus has done for us** and what Jesus can and will do for those who will repent and live for Him. **He gives us a brand-new life.**

In verse fifteen, Paul tells us to **speak forth the things of God,** to proclaim God's riches in order to **exhort everyone to give their lives to God** and to preach the glories of God to every man, woman, boy and girl. We are to **rebuke evil wherever we come across it** with all authority in the name of Jesus. Let us so live such a life that **no one has any cause to despise us**, and through us, our walk with Christ Jesus.

Chapter Two – Review Questions

1. How are the churches of today and the Cretian churches alike?

_____

_____

_____

2. The older people in the churches are, as a general rule, considered to be

_____

_____

3. A Christian who is vigilant will not be

_____

_____

_____

4. The aged Christian man must of all things be

_____

_____

_____

5. Along with a Christian love it is essential that we

_____

_____

6. Gossiping is one of the surest ways to

_____

_____

_____

7. What does the word grace mean?

_____

_____

8. The gift of salvation through the grace of God teaches us

to

_____

_____

_____

9. The phrase, "worldly lust" refers to

_____

_____

10. When Jesus died upon the cross, the veil in the temple was rent into two pieces. What did this mean?

_____

_____

_____

Chapter 3

Titus 3:1-2

¹ Put them in mind to be subject to principalities and powers, to obey magistrates, to be ready to every good work,
² To speak evil of no man, to be no brawlers, but gentle, shewing all meekness unto all men.

Paul instructs Titus to tell the Cretians that as Christians they were to be **subject to those who were in authority**. One bad habit the Cretians had was rebellion to any kind of authority. Being a true Christian meant that they were to **be in subjection to the law**, just as we are today, unless it goes against the teaching of God's Holy Word. The Cretians were opposed to anyone telling them what to do, like many people today. However, God's Word teaches us that **we are to be good citizens of our country** and communities. This way, we prove to God that we love Him and serve Him. We must **be ready to do good works before all men**.

Paul goes on to say that as Christians, we are **not to speak evil of any person**. We are not to be brawlers, argumentative, combative or prone to fight. Instead, we are to **be kind and gentle to all those around us**, having a spirit of **meekness and good will** toward all.

Titus 3:3

For we ourselves also were sometimes foolish, disobedient, deceived, serving divers lusts and pleasures, living in malice and envy, hateful, and hating one another.

Paul reminds Titus that **their own past was not so good before they met Jesus and He changed their lives.** We need to remember in dealing with sinners that **except for the grace of God, we would be the same as they**. For we have **all sinned and come short** of the glory of God.

Romans 3:23

For all have sinned, and come short of the glory of God;

This is why salvation is so important to us. For we know that **no sin can enter into heaven,** for God is holy. Either we **are saved through the shed blood of Jesus, or we are condemned by our sins** before God. Paul speaks of the unsaved, how they are foolish in all their ways without

God in their lives. Scripture teaches us that foolish people do foolish things. The world says that being crazy is **doing the same thing repeatedly while expecting a different result** each time. This is how most sinners are. They keep doing their sinful ways expecting to make heaven when they die. We know this is impossible, for **no sin or sinner can enter before God**. However, this lie is being continually repeated in churches around the world today. It makes no difference how good you may be morally, for **without a born-again experience, you are lost without God**.

Sinners deceived by Satan are disobedient to authority. They were deceived in Paul's day just as they are deceived today. Satan's tricks are still working on man. The unsaved are led by their own lust and generally are self-serving to their lust. They run after the pleasures of this world envying all of those who have more than they do. Most sinners are hateful and high-minded to those who are around them, hating those who are not subject to their own petty ways.

As we can very plainly see, this world has not changed for the better. In fact, it gets worse and worse as time goes by. The evil nature of man will remain that way until **man comes to Jesus Christ and makes Him Lord and Saviour**. For only **Jesus has the power to change the sinful nature of a sinful man**. No other "god" has the power to change man's nature. Only Jesus. Our God is the **only God who is alive and who loves us**. He teaches us to love and be compassionate with others. God does not make us serve Him. He does not make us demand that others serve Him. If we serve Him, it must be **because we desire to live for Him**.

One of the things that separates Christians from other religions is that **our God is not made of wood, stone or metal, because He is alive**. It is a shame that man's nature is continually evil, for a man who is not a born-again believer is ruled by his desires and lust for the things of this natural world. Satan has no mercy on people, driving some people to be worse than others. This is why Jesus is our only hope, because He **changes our human nature from lustful and sinful desires to worship and praise** for the one who died for us on Calvary's tree, Jesus our Saviour.

Titus 3:4-6

[4] But after that the kindness and love of God our Saviour toward man appeared,
[5] Not by works of righteousness which we have done, but according to his mercy he saved us, by the washing of regeneration, and renewing of the Holy Ghost;
[6] Which he shed on us abundantly through Jesus Christ our Saviour;

In this fourth verse, Paul talks about how the grace of God appeared unto man. Through His grace, the doors of mercy were **opened unto all mankind at the cross on Calvary**. Therefore, there is no reason why all of mankind should not be saved. The only thing they need to do is to

repent of their sins and ask Jesus into their hearts and lives. However, here is the drawback: to be saved, we must **give our will over to the Lord's control** and to take God's will for our lives. This, however, goes against man's sinful nature, since he refuses to yield himself to the power of God.

When we consider the situation, it is strange how mankind looks at his condition. **God offers us a choice, life or death**, and because of his blindness to the things of God, mankind chooses death over life rather than serve God.

If salvation could be bought, man would buy it. If it could be earned, man would do everything in his power to earn it. However, because salvation is **offered free to whosoever will**, people have decided that they do not need it or want it. Satan has blinded the eyes of people.

Verse five states: *"Not by works of righteousness which we have done, but according to his mercy he saved us."* There are **no works, good or bad, that we can do to make it into heaven**. People who try to make heaven by doing good works will never make it in. Man's righteousness **will never be enough**, which is why God has **given us mercy and grace**. By His mercy, He saved us by the **washing away of our sins through the blood of Jesus**.

Romans 10:9-10

> *⁹ That if thou shalt confess with thy mouth the Lord Jesus, and shalt believe in thine heart that God hath*

raised him from the dead, thou shalt be saved.
[10] For with the heart man believeth unto
righteousness; and with the mouth confession is
made unto salvation.

In verse six, Paul reinforces God's Word. He reminds us that **God's mercy and grace were shed upon us abundantly**. This is because of the price that Jesus Christ paid for us on the cross of Calvary. Jesus **died in our stead upon that cross to open the doors of merc**y and grace that we might be able to **go directly before God**. No longer are we separated from God's presence. No longer do we need to offer blood sacrifices before God. No longer do we need to go to a priest so he can go before God for us. Under God's grace given unto us, we can **call out to God for ourselves**.

Titus 3:7

That being justified by his grace, we should be
made heirs according to the hope of eternal life.

According to this scripture, we are **justified before God by His grace**, not of works lest any should boast. It is a gift of God, given unto us, who are saved through the blood of Jesus Christ, that we should be **heirs with Jesus in eternal life**.

Romans 8:17

And if children, then heirs; heirs of God, and joint-

heirs with Christ; if so be that we suffer with him, that we may be also glorified together.

Saints, we are **heirs of the promises of God** and **heirs to the kingdom of God**. In I Corinthians 6:19, the last part of the verse tells us that we are not our own. Then verse twenty tells us that **we are bought with a price**. That price is the shed blood of Jesus Christ. Jesus' blood paid our debt, the debt of sin. Remember the chorus that we used to sing, *He Paid a Debt He Did Not Owe*, by Ellis J. Crum. It talks about **Jesus paying a debt that we could not pay**.

When we **accept the Lord as our Saviour and Redeemer**, we are **no longer the master of our lives**, although there are some who turn their backs on God and walk away to do their own thing.

1 Corinthians 6:19-20

> *¹⁹ What? know ye not that your body is the temple of the Holy Ghost which is in you, which ye have of God, and ye are not your own?*
> *²⁰ For ye are bought with a price: therefore glorify God in your body, and in your spirit, which are God's.*

In the book of Romans, we read how we are **justified by grace in Jesus**. I have listed several scriptures below that tell us of this justification.

Romans 3:24

Being justified freely by his grace through the redemption that is in Christ Jesus:

Romans 4:24-25

24 But for us also, to whom it shall be imputed, if we believe on him that raised up Jesus our Lord from the dead;
25 Who was delivered for our offences, and was raised again for our justification.

Romans 5:1-2

1 Therefore being justified by faith, we have peace with God through our Lord Jesus Christ:
2 By whom also we have access by faith into this grace wherein we stand, and rejoice in hope of the glory of God.

How privileged we are to know Jesus as our Lord and Saviour, our Redeemer and King. We are blessed to be His servants, blessed because **when we were unlovable, He still loved us**. We are blessed that **He paid a debt we could not pay**, blessed because He **gave His life in our place** and blessed because He **made it possible that we could live eternally** with Him. Christians should all desire to be at home with Jesus.

Titus 3:8

This is a faithful saying, and these things I will that thou affirm constantly, that they which have believed in God might be careful to maintain good works. These things are good and profitable unto men.

In this eighth verse, the apostle Paul admonishes Titus to **continually preach and teach these truths** to the people in the local churches lest they forget and to **keep them in mind of God's precious promises** to His children. As we all know, the promises of God are faithful and sure to **all who believe in His grace and accept Him** as their personal Saviour.

If we are not careful, we have a tendency to forget the truths of God's Word that should be so precious to us and all of the saints of God. One of our main problems is that we get ourselves entangled in the everyday affairs of life. When we are entangled, we are **prone to get careless concerning the needs** of our spiritual man. We read our Bibles but **get in such a hurry that we get careless and do not pray for God's discernment** about what we are reading. Without God's discernment, we **do not understand** what we have been reading. Therefore, we are not truly studying God's Holy Word. Sometimes, we **let ourselves become blinded to what is right before us**.

We can become like the man who wanted to see the forest he had heard about. He became upset that he could

not see the forest because there were too many trees in the way. This may sound silly, but that is how we sometimes are. It is sad to think that many times **we cannot see what is right** in front of us. Spiritual blindness has become **an epidemic in Christian churches** around the world. The reason is that people have let Satan blind them to the truth because their **fleshly lust covers their eyes**. When we do not take the time to truly study God's Word, we **miss the blessing and promises of God** that he wants us to have. It is impossible to claim and stand upon the promises of God if we do not know what they are. Ignorance of God's Word **keeps us from the blessings that belong to us** through Jesus Christ, our Lord.

God's grace has opened the doors of heaven to us; meanwhile, we must be **faithful servants that show forth God's glory,** a servant who works for the Lord by words of witness, **revealing our Lord by works of kindness** and compassion **with love for those who** are around us. When we let our spiritual life get slack, we find ourselves walking a downward road leading away from God. I know that we get busy. However, we can **get too busy if we are not careful**. We must go to work to make a living, and we get tired. Yet, when we get home, our spouse and/or children always want something done. Finally, Sunday gets here, and we want to stay home from church so we can rest. Then, we find other things to do besides rest. God is left out of our lives, and **this is one thing that we cannot afford** to let happen. The Lord must **always come first even if we must let something** go undone. We will **never suffer**

when we put God first. His blessings are **more precious than fine gold**.

Titus 3:9

But avoid foolish questions, and genealogies, and contentions, and strivings about the law; for they are unprofitable and vain.

Verse nine goes on to instruct us as the Lord's servants **to avoid foolish questions**. The devil loves for God's servants to be an obstacle before people. One way he does this is to get us involved in questions and doctrines that serve no purpose. The more Satan can entangle us in things that do not matter, the better he likes it. We must also **be careful of double-ended questions**, questions designed to entrap us either way we answer. Here is an example: Do you spy on your neighbors before 10 o'clock or after 10 o'clock? Either way you answer, you are saying that you spy upon your neighbors. We must **be as wise as serpents and as harmless as doves**.

Matthew 10:16

Behold, I send you forth as sheep in the midst of wolves: be ye therefore wise as serpents, and harmless as doves.

I Timothy 1:4

Neither give heed to fables and endless genealogies,

*which minister questions, rather than godly edifying
which is in faith: so do.*

Foolish questions and statements are designed to
show our immaturity in the Lord and His Word. We must
remember that **we represent Jesus Christ** in this sinful
world. Always ask yourself **what Jesus would do or say** in
this situation. We must always **strive to be like Jesus**. If
we are lacking in wisdom, the Lord tells us to ask of God.

James 1:5-6

> *⁵ If any of you lack wisdom, let him ask of God, that
> giveth to all men liberally, and upbraideth not; and
> it shall be given him.*
> *⁶ But let him ask in faith, nothing wavering. For he
> that wavereth is like a wave of the sea driven with
> the wind and tossed.*

At times, living for Christ and **staying true to the
Christian example** presented to us by Paul can seem an
impossible task. Who can do such a thing without falling
into despair, if we must always be spotless before the
world? However, when we **truly live for the Lord**, we find
it a pleasure, knowing that **we are never alone** and that
Jesus is **always with us,** helping us to overcome the trials
of life. Some will say that I am trying to make living for
God too hard, but **it is God and the Bible that sets our
standards**. When we follow God's plan, we will discover

that **living for God has its own rewards**.

The scripture tells us to **avoid genealogies, contentions, and strivings about the law**. In the early Christian churches, the Jews loved to bring up their family histories and talk about how far back they could trace their family trees. To the Jews, tracing their family's genealogy was very important; it was a matter of pride to them and showed that they, the Jews, were **more important to God than any Gentile**. The Jews took great pleasure in taunting the Gentile Christians and stirring up contentions among the congregation members. They continually kept trying to **bring the law into their worship services**. This repeatedly angered the Gentile Christians. Remember, the devil will stop at nothing to destroy the church of God. **Contention about small matters that do not affect our relationship with God must be put away and not allowed to impact our Christian relationship with our fellow believers.**

II Timothy 2:23-24

> [23] *But foolish and unlearned questions avoid, knowing that they do gender strifes.*
> [24] *And the servant of the Lord must not strive; but be gentle unto all men, apt to teach, patient,*

Paul goes on to say such things were unimportant and vain. **Stirring up problems is not an acceptable Christian pastime.** You have heard people say someone was making a mountain out of a molehill. This is what

Satan loves to do to us, to make **unimportant things seem to be the most important things,** all to get us caught up in needless affairs. Thus, we are distracted from what is important. **Deception is one of the greatest weapons that the devil uses against the Christian people today.**

Titus 3:10-11

[10] A man that is an heretick after the first and second admonition reject;
[11] Knowing that he that is such is subverted, and sinneth, being condemned of himself.

Never before has the church world seen so many heretics in the church. What is a heretic?

Webster's New World College Dictionary states:

Heretic: a church member who holds beliefs opposed to church dogma

Barnes' Notes on the New Testament adds:

A man that is an heretic. The word heretic is now commonly applied to one who holds some fundamental error of doctrine, "a person who holds and teaches opinions repugnant to the established faith, or that which is made the standard of orthodoxy".

In today's world, there are heretics coming out of the woodwork, so to speak. Heretics are people who **hold ideas and beliefs that are opposite to the true teachings** of the scriptures. All you have to do is listen to the radio or television at what some ministers and teachers are preaching and teaching. Some **refuse to preach and teach against sin**. Some **refuse to take a stand for God**.

Today, I read about an Anglican Bishop who wrote to her fellow ministers that they should no longer preach or teach that God is male. They should not refer to God as He or Him, since it might hinder women in their service of God. Here is a perfect example of being a heretic. The scriptures teach us that God is male; the scriptures tells us that **God is a He or Him, and Jesus tells us that God is His Father.** A father can only be male.

In a world that is opposed to the Christian faith and a church world that is so liberal that it no longer holds to the true doctrine of Christ, the **fundamental Christians have their backs against the wall**. The church world is so cowardly as a whole that they now let the world dictate what the morals of the church are to be. In their opinion, to preach *thus sayeth the Lord* is no longer acceptable since it **goes against popular belief and opinion**.

Paul goes on to say that such a person should be admonished once and if need be, twice. Then, if there was no change, the church was to reject that person. The ministry and the local congregation were to reject them. The church **could not afford to have such a person in their congregation continually causing confusion and tur-**

moil. The rejection was to be public so that all might know what had happened and why. To do so secretly would only cause more confusion and rumors to abound, and this would fit right into the devil's plans.

We cannot depend on gossip and rumors to be the truth. Remember the game of "Rumor" or "Gossip" that was so popular at parties, the one where you had several people sit in a circle, then you whispered a secret into one person's ear, and each person passed it on to the next? When it had gone all the way around the circle, the last person told what they heard. What came out was usually not what was said in the beginning. **Do not believe rumors or gossip.**

Know that a heretic has been subverted by the devil, that he or she **sins willfully and is condemned** by his or her own doings. The sad thing is that he or she also **leads many of their followers astray and down a sinful road** toward a devil's hell.

Titus 3:12-13

¹² When I shall send Artemas unto thee, or Tychicus, be diligent to come unto me to Nicopolis: for I have determined there to winter.
¹³ Bring Zenas the lawyer and Apollos on their journey diligently, that nothing be wanting unto them.

Paul, in this twelfth verse, is telling Titus that

88

sometime in the very near future, he was going to send Artemis to replace him at Crete. However, if Artemis could not go, then he would send Tychicus in his place. As best as can be determined, it was Artemis who replaced Titus in Crete.

Who was Artemis? No one knows for sure. He just **appears and then just as quickly disappears** back into history, no longer to be heard. After Artemis arrived, Titus was to go to Nicopolis to meet Paul, since that was where Paul was going to spend the winter. He wanted Titus there with him.

Paul, in verse thirteen, tells Titus that when he comes to Nicopolis to **bring certain ones with him**. He was to bring Zenas, the lawyer. Along with Zenas, he was to bring Apollos, since **Paul had need of them both**. Because of the Roman persecution, they were to be diligently careful on their journey. Paul goes on to say that they were to **want for nothing on their journey**. It was the custom for the local churches to help travelers along their way. They provided **food and shelter**, and just as importantly, **information to travelers** on their journeys.

Titus 3:14-15

[14] And let ours also learn to maintain good works for necessary uses, that they be not unfruitful.
[15] All that are with me salute thee. Greet them that love us in the faith. Grace be with you all. Amen.

In verse fourteen Paul tells us that he is hoping that all Christians will **learn to maintain good works and that it is our duty to help meet the needs of our brothers** and sisters in Christ. We should help them with their needs in the natural, and above that, **provide for their spiritual needs**. When we do so, we **prove ourselves fruitful before God**.

In verse fifteen, Paul gives salutations to Titus and all of those who are with him. He also tells Titus to give greetings to **all of those who love him and his fellow laborers**. Then he **speaks the grace of God to all of them**.

Amen
(It is finished)

Chapter Three – Review Questions

1. What was one bad habit that the Cretians had?

_____

_____

2. Our God is the only God who is

_____

_____

3. What do we need to do, to be saved or born again?

_____

_____

_____

4. Too many times we are prone to get careless concerning

_____

_____

5. It is impossible to stand upon the promises of God when

_____

_____

_____

6. What are foolish questions and statements designed to do?

_____

_____

_____

7. What does *Webster's Dictionary* say a heretic is?

_____

_____

_____

8. Who did Paul send to replace Titus?

_____

_____

_____

9. Where was Paul planning on spending the winter?

_____

_____

_____

The Book of

Philemon

Introduction to Philemon

Philemon was a well-to-do member of the church in Colossae. It is believed that Philemon was the owner of Onesimus, a runaway slave. Onesimus, having been converted to Christianity, was being returned to Philemon.

From Paul's letter, it is thought that Philemon was a leader of the Colossian church. Paul himself led Philemon to Jesus Christ. Information suggests that Philemon became the bishop of Colossae. Tradition also tells us that Philemon, his wife, son and faithful slave Onesimus were stoned to death during Nero's reign.

Chapter 1

¹ Paul, a prisoner of Jesus Christ, and Timothy our brother, unto Philemon our dearly beloved, and fellowlabourer,
² And to our beloved Apphia, and Archippus our fellowsoldier, and to the church in thy house:
³ Grace to you, and peace, from God our Father and the Lord Jesus Christ.
⁴ I thank my God, making mention of thee always in my prayers,

Paul, as usual, begins this letter to Philemon by telling the reader who he is, Paul, a prisoner of Jesus Christ. One of the things we should love about Paul is **his humbleness and his meekness**. He always proclaimed his reverence to his Lord and his **submission to God's will** in his life. Paul did not boast of himself. He always **gave glory and honor to our Lord**.

Paul, in this first verse, calls himself a prisoner of

Jesus Christ. In a time of servitude, Paul well knew what it meant to be a prisoner. When he surrendered to Jesus Christ, he **considered himself a prisoner of the Lord**, a prisoner of love. In his address, he also mentions that Timothy is with him. Then he addresses Philemon as **his beloved fellow laborer** in Jesus Christ.

In verse two, Paul addresses those who are with Philemon. First, he addresses *"our beloved Apphia."* It is believed by his greeting that Apphia was Philemon's wife and companion in the ministry. Archippus is believed to be Philemon and Apphia's son. It is also believed that Archippus was a minister in the local church that met in their home. To this church, Paul **gives greetings of grace and peace in the name** of Jesus Christ. In the early days of the church, most believers met in private homes.

In verse four, Paul goes on to tell them that he **thinks of them often and prays for them**, and he asks that the grace and blessings of God will rest upon them. Scripture tells us to **pray one for another, which is our duty** in our service of the Lord. As Christians, we are to pray for **sinners to be saved**, to pray for **our families**, and to pray for **our churches and our friends**. Paul sets us an example we do well to follow.

James 5:16

> *Confess your faults one to another, and pray one for another, that ye may be healed. The effectual fervent prayer of a righteous man availeth much.*

Philemon 1:5-7

⁵ Hearing of thy love and faith, which thou hast toward the Lord Jesus, and toward all saints;
⁶ That the communication of thy faith may become effectual by the acknowledging of every good thing which is in you in Christ Jesus.
⁷ For we have great joy and consolation in thy love, because the bowels of the saints are refreshed by thee, brother.

In verse five, Paul makes mention of the faith of Philemon and his family, of how they **trust in Jesus as their Lord and Saviour** and how they are **committed to their fellow saints** in the Lord. Philemon is a perfect example of what a pastor should be, **giving of himself to the work of Jesus and the message** of the gospel, showing that by the **witnessing of our faith in Jesus Christ**, we might **lead others to the Lord**. It makes me wonder what Paul would think of how we live our lives today. If we are to become effectual in our service for Jesus Christ, we must **live our lives in accordance with God's Word**. We must acknowledge our Lord in everything we do. Our lives must **continually give praise and glory** to Jesus Christ. We must so live that the lost sinners of this world can see the love of Jesus in us. We are to be the **Lord's hand extended**. We are living in the last days before Jesus comes back for His church. We must **reach as many of the lost** as we can, now **before it is too late**.

In verse seven we read, *"For we have great joy and consolation in thy love."* In thy love means **his love toward his fellow brothers** and sisters in the Lord. *"*B*ecause the bowels of the saints are refreshed by thee, brother."* The word *bowels* means their minds or their hearts.

Barnes' Notes on the New Testament tells us:

> *Because the bowels of the saints are refreshed by thee, brother.* For your kindness to them. The word *bowels* here probably means *minds, hearts,* for it is used in the Scriptures to denote the affections. The sense is that the kindness which he had shown to Christians had done much to make them happy.

This is what a good pastor is supposed to do, to give **comfort to those who are in distress**, to those who are overcome by the problems of this life. A pastor's work is to **build their faith through the words of our Lord**, speaking **love and peace and contentment**, words that soothe the troubled soul and give hope to the soul.

Philemon 1:8-9

⁸ Wherefore, though I might be much bold in Christ
to enjoin thee that which is convenient,
⁹ Yet for love's sake I rather beseech thee, being

such an one as Paul the aged, and now also a
prisoner of Jesus Christ.

Paul begins this ninth verse by saying, *"Yet for love's sake I rather beseech thee."* Paul is saying that **because of their common love in Christ Jesus**, he was asking them to please hear his request and honor it **as coming from Jesus Christ**.

Barnes' Notes on the New Testament gives us insight to Paul's intent:

> The apostle implies here that what he was about to ask was *proper to be done* in the circumstances, but he does not put it on that ground, but rather asks it as a personal favour. It is usually not best to *command* a thing to be done, if we can as well secure it by asking it as a favour.

Paul refers to himself as *"Paul the aged."* He was confessing that he was an old man. No one knows how old Paul was at this time. It is believed that Paul was somewhere between fifty and sixty years of age. Paul's body was aged because of what we would call "wear and tear" due to what he went through in his service for the Lord. Remember that he **suffered in prison and was often mistreated,** even **stoned at one point**. Then he was shipwrecked. Even so, he considered the **harshness of his**

101

Christian walk part of his service for Jesus Christ, his Lord and Master.

Philemon 1:10-13

[10] *I beseech thee for my son Onesimus, whom I have begotten in my bonds:*
[11] *Which in time past was to thee unprofitable, but now profitable to thee and to me:*
[12] *Whom I have sent again: thou therefore receive him, that is, mine own bowels:*
[13] *Whom I would have retained with me, that in thy stead he might have ministered unto me in the bonds of the gospel:*

Paul, in this tenth verse, is telling Philemon, his good friend and fellow laborer in the Lord Jesus Christ, that he, Paul, is petitioning Philemon to **let his love of the Lord and the saints to be in control of his life** and emotions and to have **Christian love and compassion upon his runaway slave**, Onesimus. Paul calls Onesimus **his son in the bonds of love**. Paul did not want Philemon to revert in his mind to the time when Onesimus was an unruly and disobedient slave that had run away.

I want to compare the King James Version and the Interlinear Greek Version of verse ten to illustrate a vital nuance in how Paul pleaded with Philemon for Onesimus' sake.

Philemon 1:10 (KJV)

[10] I beseech thee for my son Onesimus, whom I have begotten in my bonds:

The Greek translation turns this around, putting **what Paul has done for Onesimus before recognizing the runaway slave** by name:

Philemon 1:10 (IGV)

[10] I am calling you ... about my offspring whom I generated... Onesimus! (added exclamation point)

You can see the difference. Paul wants to **explain his position,** and he makes it clear that **he would do the same for any Christian brother** in Onesimus' place! Now let's add another layer of clarification using *Barnes' Notes.*

Barnes' Notes on the New Testament explains:

> In the original, the name Onesimus is reserved to come in last in the sentence. The order of the Greek is this: "I entreat thee concerning a son of mine, whom I have begotten in my bonds-Onesimus." Here the name is not suggested, until he had mentioned that he sustained to him the relation of a son, and also till he had added

that his conversion was the fruit of his labours *while he was a prisoner*. Then, when the name of Onesimus is mentioned, it would occur to Philemon not primarily as the name of an ungrateful and disobedient servant, but as the interesting case of one converted by the labours of his own friend in prison. Was there ever more delicacy evinced in preparing the way for disarming one of prejudice, and carrying an appeal to his heart?

After Onesimus ran away from Philemon's household, **somewhere he encountered Paul**. The scriptures give us very little information in this area. I would venture to say that Onesimus came across Paul preaching the gospel message of Jesus Christ and His salvation, a salvation that was **freely given to all, rich or poor, bond or free**. It made no difference who you were, man or woman. As Onesimus inquired about this salvation that would set a person free, Paul was able to **witness to him on a personal basis about the love** and mercy of Jesus Christ. Onesimus gave his heart and life over to Jesus as his Lord and Saviour, and after his conversion, his **whole life was changed**. He turned around completely. He became a **constant help to Paul and the ministry** of the gospel.

Paul goes on to tell Philemon that at one time Onesimus was unprofitable to him; however, his heart has been **changed by the Lord**. Paul says that Onesimus was now **very profitable to him and that he would be very profitable to Philemon**. Paul further goes on to tell Philemon that he was sending Onesimus back to him. Paul asks Philemon to **receive Onesimus as a brother in the Lord** and not as a runaway slave, which Philemon did for all to see.

Philemon 1:14-16

14 But without thy mind would I do nothing; that thy benefit should not be as it were of necessity, but willingly.
15 For perhaps he therefore departed for a season, that thou shouldest receive him for ever;
16 Not now as a servant, but above a servant, a brother beloved, specially to me, but how much more unto thee, both in the flesh, and in the Lord?

Paul, in the fourteenth verse, expresses his difficulty in making his decision about what he was going to do about Onesimus. On one hand, Paul **wanted to keep Onesimus as his coworker**, as his **assistant in the ministry of the gospel**. Paul often took young converts under his wing and instructed them in the teachings of the gospel. This is what Paul wanted to do with Onesimus. Yet, to keep Onesimus as his assistant and student **was to do wrong to Philemon**. Since Onesimus was the property of his good friend Philemon, and **according to Roman law, Onesimus had to be returned** to his master. With Paul being a Roman citizen, he had a responsibility to return Onesimus. So, as Paul writes this letter to Philemon, he tells Philemon that the **decision of what to do about Onesimus was up to him**.

Paul continues in verse fifteen saying that perhaps it was in the will of God that Onesimus ran away. By running away, he was **exposed to a life of always looking behind him** to see if someone was in pursuit of him. In his difficulties, he heard Paul preach the gospel and **received Jesus as his Saviour**, thus becoming a **member of the Christian family and a brother in Christ** to his master.

Paul goes on to say in verse sixteen that Onesimus was returning not only as a servant, but **also as more than a servant**. Onesimus was returning **as a brother in Christ**. Paul states that **as a brother in Christ, Onesimus was very special to him** and he would be the same to Philemon. He would be special in the flesh (or everyday living) and in the Lord as a **Christian brother in the service of God**.

Philemon 1:17-18

17 If thou count me therefore a partner, receive him as myself.
18 If he hath wronged thee, or oweth thee ought, put that on mine account;

Paul tells Philemon that if he counts Paul as a partner (or a brother in Christ Jesus), he was asking him to **receive Onesimus the same as he would receive Paul**. In other words, extend to him **every kindness as unto the Lord**. Christians were to **show hospitality to travelers and other Christians**, something that is not being taught in churches today. What a shame to Christians!

In verse eighteen, Paul tells Philemon that if Onesimus has wronged him or if he owes him anything to put it on Paul's account, that Paul **would take all of the responsibility for any wrongdoing** that had been done unto Philemon.

Philemon 1:19

I Paul have written it with mine own hand, I will repay it: albeit I do not say to thee how thou owest unto me even thine own self besides.

In this verse, Philemon learns that Paul took the time to **write this letter with his own hand**. This was unusual as Paul usually had someone to write his letters as he dictated them. **For Paul to take the time to sit down and write this letter himself was a great show of his favor and affection for Philemon.**

Paul again tells Philemon that he will stand good for Onesimus if he owes anything. Paul further states that he is not saying that Philemon owes him anything, because Paul was the one who led Philemon to the Lord.

Philemon 1:20-22

[20] Yea, brother, let me have joy of thee in the Lord:

refresh my bowels in the Lord.
²¹ Having confidence in thy obedience I wrote unto thee, knowing that thou wilt also do more than I say.
²² But withal prepare me also a lodging: for I trust that through your prayers I shall be given unto you.

Paul is stating, *"let me have joy of thee in the Lord."* This was Paul's way of asking Philemon to **honor his request concerning Onesimus**, his friend and brother in Jesus Christ. Paul was an iconic figure respected by all of the Christian community and looked up to as an apostle of the Lord Jesus Christ. **If Philemon granted Paul's request, Paul would see it as the will of the Lord.**

In verse twenty-one, Paul is saying that he has all confidence in what Philemon would do, believing that Philemon would do as he requested and even more than he asked for. We, as brothers and sisters in Christ, need to **be helpful to each other**. For **only Christians can understand what other Christians go through** in the true service of Jesus Christ. The world does not understand our sacrifice in serving the Lord, nor can they, not having had a personal experience with Jesus.

Paul in this next verse asks Philemon to prepare a place for him to stay. For it was his intention, the Lord permitting, to come and stay with Philemon for a while.

Philemon 1:23-25

²³ There salute thee Epaphras, my fellowprisoner in Christ Jesus;
²⁴ Marcus, Aristarchus, Demas, Lucas, my fellowlabourers.
²⁵ The grace of our Lord Jesus Christ be with your spirit. Amen.

In closing his letter to Philemon, Paul acknowledges those who were with him. First, there was Epaphras, whom Paul calls my fellow-prisoner in Christ Jesus. Then, in verse twenty-four, Paul goes on to mention the others who were with him. Their names were Marcus, Aristarchus, Demas, and Lucas, men in the service of God. (Aside, even as the disciples were with Jesus, and Judas turned his back on Jesus, soon Paul would find Demas to be like Judas. Demas would come to the point of leaving the ministry and going back into the world.)

In the last verse, Paul ends by asking the grace of Jesus Christ to rest upon Philemon.

In closing, let me recap what we can glean from the book of Philemon. Onesimus asked Paul to send him back to Philemon of his own free will. Onesimus became a faithful servant to Philemon. Tradition maintains that Philemon, his wife Apphia, son Archippus and his beloved and faithful slave Onesimus were all stoned to death for their stand and belief in Jesus Christ.

Chapter One – Review Questions

1. What did Paul always proclaim?

_____

_____

_____

2. Who does Paul acknowledge was with him?

_____

_____

_____

3. Who is believed to be Philemon's son?

_____

_____

_____

4. Paul is asking Philemon to have Christian love and compassion upon whom?

_____

_____

_____

5. Why, by keeping Onesimus as his co-worker, was Paul doing Philemon wrong?

_____

_____

_____

6. What did Roman law dictate about runaway slaves?

_____

_____

_____

Bibliography

Rev. John Phillips
> *The John Phillips Commentary Series*
> Kregel Publications
> Grand Rapids, Michigan
> Published 2001

Rev. Albert Barnes
> *Barnes' Notes on the New Testament*
> Baker Book House Company
> Grand Rapids, Michigan
> Reprinted 2005
> Reprinted from the 1847 edition published by
>> Blackie & Son, London

Webster's New World College Dictionary
> IDG Books Worldwide Inc.
> An International Data Group Company
> Foster City, California
> Fourth Edition
> Copyright 2000

Scripture for All
> **Greek / Hebrew Interlinear Bible**
> Greek and Hebrew Interlinears
> Copyright 2020 Scripture4All Publishing
> https://www.scripture4all.org/

Answers to Review Questions

Titus

Chapter 1 (page 40)

1. The promises are to God's children, all born again believers, the saints.
2. The book of Ecclesiastes written by Solomon. Ecclesiastes 3:1
3. The belief in Jesus Christ as our personal Lord and Saviour.
4. Titus was to *"set in order the things that were wanting."*
5. The setting of rules of conduct and rules of order for the church to follow.
6. Being holy is to live according to the principles of God's Word.
7. For us through His power, to be in control of our emotions and desires.
8. The Cretians (Cretans) originally came Asia Minor.
9. He was to rebuke them sharply in the matter of serving God.

Chapter 2 (page 70)

1. They were and we are today constantly under attack

from all sides.

2. The foundation of the church.
3. Found doing the will of the devil.
4. Sound in the doctrine of faith in Jesus Christ.
5. Have patience with the world around us.
6. Spread discord among the members of the church.
7. It means unmerited favor.
8. To live godly in this present world.
9. All improper desires pertaining to this life.
10. This signified that no longer was man separated from God.

Chapter 3 (page 91)

1. The Cretians were rebellious to any kind of authority.
2. Alive
3. Repent of our sins and ask Jesus into our hearts and lives.
4. The needs of our spiritual man.
5. When we do not know what they are.
6. They are designed to show our immaturity in the Lord and His Word.
7. A Church member who holds beliefs opposed to church dogma.
8. Artemis or Tychicus
9. Nicopolis

Philemon

Chapter 1 (page 110)

1. Paul proclaimed his love and reverence.
2. Timothy
3. Archippus
4. His runaway slave, Onesimus
5. Because Onesimus was the property of Philemon
6. They must be returned to their master or owners.

Coming Soon!

A Study on I and II Timothy

Introduction

Timothy was one of the favorite companions of Paul. In the circle of saints that Paul mentions by name, Timothy stands out repeatedly. Paul addressed two of his epistles to Timothy, as well as naming Timothy sixteen times in his gospels. Paul spent time grooming (or training) Timothy for the ministry that lay ahead. Many believe that Paul was preparing Timothy to take his place when God called him home. Timothy was some twenty years old when Paul gave him the opportunity to act on his own, creating a separate identity from Paul. Paul sent Timothy from Athens to Thessalonica to complete the work of organizing the church there. Paul spoke of Timothy as doing the same work that Paul did.

1 Corinthians 16:10

Now if Timotheus come, see that he may be with you without fear: for he worketh the work of the Lord, as I also do.

In the twenty years of Timothy's life recorded in the New Testament, Timothy spent much of his time in missionary journeys or on missions for his friend, Paul.

What stands out about Timothy is that **he was a peace-loving man with a very humble heart**. It could be said of him that he had a pastor's heart.

Now let us look at the question of whether Timothy was an apostle in his own right or if his service in the ministry was that of a deputy apostleship to Paul. In Paul's letter to the Thessalonians, Paul names **Silvanus and Timothy along with himself as equals** in the apostleship of Christ. Timothy may seem to be a minor apostle alongside a major figure like Paul. Nevertheless, Timothy **carried out an apostolic ministry, making the answer an unqualified yes**. Timothy's selfless and repeated sacrifices for Christ **firmly establish him in the annals of the Word** as an apostle in his own right.

We know that Timothy was raised in a Godly home. Paul in II Timothy 3:15 tells of Timothy **knowing the scriptures from his childhood**. Paul also speaks of Timothy's **steadfast faith**, and not just Timothy alone. He includes his grandmother, Lois, and his mother, Eunice. These two women **instilled in Timothy a faith in God which was to last him throughout his life**. Nothing is known of Timothy's father, save that he was a Greek Gentile. Like all Gentiles, he must have refused to let Timothy be circumcised, something Timothy's mother believed in, being a Jew.

When Timothy joined Paul in his work for the Lord, Timothy quickly found out that **the Gentiles would listen to his message of Christ, while the Jews, on the other hand, would turn away from him** because he was not

120

circumcised. Listening to Paul, Timothy underwent the painful operation of circumcision for the sake of the gospel. Afterwards, Timothy could **minister to both the Gentiles and the Jews**.

Paul and Timothy labored together for the Lord. Paul states that **Timothy was his son in the Lord** Jesus Christ. Together on missionary journeys, they **suffered together and were even in peril many times**. Paul instructed Timothy to make **full proof of his ministry by doing the work of an evangelist** to preach and spread the message of our Lord and Saviour Jesus Christ.

Timothy was not another Paul. His ministry was more of a caretaker. The major apostles blazed the trail. They started the churches, and those who came after them served as apostles in their own right. It was up to them to complete the work that the major apostles had started. Timothy was charged with the **responsibility of correcting backsliding churches, reproving, rebuking with all long-suffering to soothe the saints** in times of trouble, and to **encourage and lift up the churches as well as lead the lost to Jesus**.

Paul sent to Timothy, his spiritual son, two letters (or epistles). In the first letter, Timothy is told to **preach the truth and to preach it straight**. Secondly, he is told to **guard the truth of the doctrine of Christ**, which is the message of salvation without which no one can be saved. Timothy also is told to **guard his testimony**, his witness, since there would come some who would try to besmirch or make dirty his life's work since the devil is our adversary and will do all in his power to destroy our witness. Paul's warning was to be careful and to let no man beguile him. He encouraged Timothy to be **bold because the love of many would wax cold**. The last that we know of Timothy is that he was still serving God. How and where he died, no one knows.

Chapter One

1 Timothy 1:1

Paul, an apostle of Jesus Christ by the commandment of God our Saviour, and Lord Jesus Christ, which is our hope;

Paul, in writing the first epistle, starts out by addressing who he was and telling his title. In this way, there would be **no mistake about who wrote this epistle or letter**. This letter was not a personal letter written only to Timothy but was **meant to be read to the whole body of believers**. For this reason, we call these letters of I and II Timothy and some others *pastoral epistles*. It is believed that Timothy was pastoring one of the churches in Ephesus when Paul wrote this letter to him.

Another commonly held belief is that Paul had sent Timothy to Ephesus to take charge and straighten out some serious problems that had come upon the church. In the book of Acts, Paul had warned the people in the church of

Ephesus that after he left, "grievous wolves" would come into the church to destroy it.

Acts 20:28-32

> [28] *Take heed therefore unto yourselves, and to all the flock, over the which the Holy Ghost hath made you overseers, to feed the church of God, which he hath purchased with his own blood.*
> [29] *For I know this, that after my departing shall grievous wolves enter in among you, not sparing the flock.*
> [30] *Also of your own selves shall men arise, speaking perverse things, to draw away disciples after them.*
> [31] *Therefore watch, and remember, that by the space of three years I ceased not to warn every one night and day with tears.*
> [32] *And now, brethren, I commend you to God, and to the word of his grace, which is able to build you up, and to give you an inheritance among all them which are sanctified.*

It was for this reason that Timothy was sent to the church in Ephesus. He was sent to try to **restore order and a Christ-like spirit in the church** and lives of the people. Somehow, Timothy became the pastor of the church. Paul also wanted to give him guidance in **how to handle the situations that were transpiring** in the church. By Paul addressing the letter the way he did, Paul was giving

Timothy the authority to **do what was needed as though Paul was there himself**. It had been only seven years since Paul had praised the church at Ephesus for their stand for Christ. How quickly the enemy can do harm when we fail to be on guard.

In the world in which we live, though many have fallen by the wayside, there is **divine hope for those that are lost**. It is important to remember that Paul was an apostle of the Lord Jesus Christ by the commandment of God our Saviour and the Lord Jesus Christ, who is our eternal hope. That commandment **still applies to Christians in the 21st century**. Paul is now in heaven, but the **message of hope and love that he preached remains** with us. We are the **heirs of the apostle's ministry**. The apostles of old are all gone, but we are left, and we are **all called to be witnesses for Christ**. It is up to us to carry on the message that God loves people. He cares where souls are going to spend eternity. It is up to us to **spread the good news** to all who will listen that Jesus saves and **there is hope through His powerful name**.

It is not too late to reach out to your friends and family before Jesus comes. We can never **give up hope for our loved ones and friends**. To give up hope is to condemn souls to an eternity without God. **As long as there is breath, there is hope.** As long as there is breath, there is still a chance that **souls will humble themselves before God** and repent. If we give up, then who will pray for our lost love ones? If we refuse to give of ourselves, I can assure you that there is no one who will take our place. **No**

one can fill your place in the Kingdom of God, and no one can fill your place here on earth. If Paul had said no to God's call two thousand years ago, where would the church be today? **Thank God Paul said yes** to the **calling that was placed before him**.

To understand the lives of the apostles and what they sacrificed to serve the Lord, it is important that we remember that in their world, especially the part controlled by Rome, it was a very dangerous place for Christians to live. Satan used the Roman Empire in his plans to attempt to destroy the growing church of Jesus Christ. Never, never let us forget **where God has brought us from** and **where we are headed**, to a home on high with Jesus our Lord and Saviour, our Redeemer, our soon-coming King.

1 Timothy 1:2

Unto Timothy, my own son in the faith: Grace, mercy, and peace, from God our Father and Jesus Christ our Lord.

In this second verse, Paul addresses the letter to Timothy. Timothy was in Ephesus because Paul had sent him there to **take charge and to put an end to the trouble that had arisen** in the church. Paul addresses Timothy as **his son in the faith**. Paul felt like he was Timothy's spiritual father and took the steps that he felt necessary to **see Timothy grow in the love and grace of God** and Jesus Christ. Timothy, it appears, had done just that, because

Paul now **trusted Timothy's ability and maturity**, or he would not have sent him to Ephesus.

It is commonly believed that Timothy was somewhere around fifteen years old when Paul first came to Lystra to preach the gospel of Jesus Christ. It is understood that **Timothy was saved on Paul's first missionary journey** to Lystra or shortly thereafter. On Paul's second journey to Lystra, **he and Timothy became fast friends**, a friendship that would last all of their lives. Timothy, after becoming friends with Paul, **began traveling with him on many of his missionary journeys**. Timothy is believed to be about twenty years of age at this time.

As Paul and Timothy traveled together, we can only imagine the wealth of wisdom that Paul imparted to Timothy. We can be sure Paul told Timothy about his experience on the road to Damascus and about how Jesus had talked to him and called him to be a witness to the lost souls of the world. He certainly shared how his ministry was to be mostly to the Gentiles, and how Paul wanted to teach Timothy to do the Lord's work in spreading the gospel of Jesus Christ. **Timothy learned well and became an apostle along with Paul and the others.** Timothy became **pastor of the Ephesus church** and was about thirty- to thirty-five years of age when Paul wrote this first apostle to him. This epistle was to **both Timothy and the church**.

1 Timothy 1:3-4

³ As I besought thee to abide still at Ephesus, when I went into Macedonia, that thou mightest charge some that they teach no other doctrine,
⁴ Neither give heed to fables and endless genealogies, which minister questions, rather than godly edifying which is in faith: so do.

In these verses, we see that Paul had to leave Ephesus to go into Macedonia on some business for the Lord. We know that Paul and Timothy worked together for the Lord in many places. Yet, in this matter, Paul told Timothy that it was **needful for Timothy to stay in Ephesus to complete the work** in progress there. One of the main problems in the church was the false beliefs that were propagated by many in the churches there. The church at Ephesus was **one of the leading churches in the area**. If the church at Ephesus became doctrinally unsound, **other churches would certainly follow** their lead.

Timothy was charged to see that **no erroneous doctrine was taught**. Paul also warns against believing in fables and people's misconceptions about the gospels. It is important that we **keep the truth before the saints of God**. To do this we must **keep Christian workers who are rooted and grounded** in the Word of God. There are far too many so-called Christians today who have a form of godliness but deny the power thereof. A form of godliness is very dangerous to the saints of God. Satan loves to lead the saints of God astray by bringing in falsehoods. For this reason, the saints of God need to be **grounded in the true** doctrine of the gospel. When I say gospel, I mean the **full gospel, the whole Word of God**. God does not give us the right to pick and choose what we want to believe. Should someone choose to believe only parts of God's Word, then why believe any of it? Believe **all of it or none of it**. God's Word teaches us to be **either hot or cold**, because if we are lukewarm, He will spew us out of His mouth.

Revelation 3:15-16

> [15] *I know thy works, that thou art neither cold nor hot: I would thou wert cold or hot.*
> [16] *So then because thou art lukewarm, and neither cold nor hot, I will spue thee out of my mouth.*

In too many churches around the world today, you will find that they have become places of entertainment where the creature is praised and magnified far more than the creator. So, what is the problem? The problem is when we do not teach and preach the true doctrine of the gospel of Jesus Christ. We will be led astray by the enemy, which is the devil.

The John Phillips Commentary Series – Exploring the Pastoral Epistles, speaks on this issue:

> The story is told of a woman and her child who were traveling by train across the prairies in subzero weather. The woman kept on

anxiously looking about her, worried about missing her stop. The conductor assured her that he would see her off the train at the right stop. A fellow traveler, a salesman, also tried to reassure her. "I travel this line frequently, lady," he said. "I know every station and whistle-stop. If the conductor forgets, I'll make sure you get off at the right place."

Soon the salesman said, "Yours will be the next stop." After a while the train came to a halt. There was no sign of the conductor. "This is where you get off, lady. I'll help you out with your bags."

It was dark and snowing hard, and there was no one in sight. The fellow passenger assured the frightened woman, "They'll have heard the train. They'll be along in a minute. This has to be your stop." He climbed back on board as the train pulled away.

Several minutes later, the conductor came through the car. "Where's the lady with the child?" he asked.

"I helped her off at the last stop," said the salesman. "That was her stop and you weren't here."

"That was not a station!" cried the conductor. "We were held up by a signal. There are no houses for miles around." The engineer stopped the train and backed it up. They found the woman and her child frozen to death. They were victims of false information.

People who teach false doctrine are as dangerous as that salesman. And people who listen to such teachers are in dire peril. So it was important for Timothy to put a stop to the propagation of false doctrine.

Many people try to show themselves to be more than what they are. They try to show how much they know about the Bible and scriptures by spouting off legends that they have learned. And some of this is believed by gullible Christians. Fellow Christians, **do not believe anything that cannot be backed up by scripture**, and never, ever take the scriptures out of context. The doctrine of Jesus Christ, the Christian doctrine, has no place for disagreements espoused by the worldly-minded people who are as carnal in nature as not to know the Spirit of God.

1 Timothy 1:5-7

⁵ Now the end of the commandment is charity out of a pure heart, and of a good conscience, and of faith unfeigned:
⁶ From which some having swerved have turned aside unto vain jangling;
⁷ Desiring to be teachers of the law; understanding neither what they say, nor whereof they affirm.

Paul begins these scriptures by saying that *"the end of the commandment is charity out of a pure heart."* Charity is **most often called love**, and the scriptures tell us **to love one another**.

John 13:34-35

> *[34] A new commandment I give unto you, That ye love one another; as I have loved you, that ye also love one another.*
> *[35] By this shall all men know that ye are my disciples, if ye have love one to another.*

If we love one another, then it is easier to keep God's Ten Commandments. Love is **caring about those around you**. We as Christians are told by scripture to have **a Christ-like love for everyone**. We do not have to lend our approval to the way people live or the things that they do. Still, we must **have a love for their eternal souls**. You, my friends, must learn to separate the way that people live (or their sinful lifestyle) from their souls. To make it plainer, **hate the sin that people do but love the sinner**. Love their souls, for this natural body will decay and vanish away, but **the soul lives forever**.

In verse six, Paul is writing about some Christians turning from the truth (in other words, backsliding) and just plain walking away from God and all He has to offer. Yes, people can backslide and lose out with God, and yes, a person who dies in a backslid condition will go to hell.

Ezekiel 18:24

But when the righteous turneth away from his righteousness, and committeth iniquity, and doeth according to all the abominations that the wicked man doeth, shall he live? All his righteousness that he hath done shall not be mentioned: in his trespass that he hath trespassed, and in his sin that he hath sinned, in them shall he die.

2 Peter 2:20-22

[20] For if after they have escaped the pollutions of the world through the knowledge of the Lord and Saviour Jesus Christ, they are again entangled therein, and overcome, the latter end is worse with them than the beginning.
[21] For it had been better for them not to have known the way of righteousness, than, after they have known it, to turn from the holy commandment delivered unto them.
[22] But it is happened unto them according to the true proverb, The dog is turned to his own vomit again; and the sow that was washed to her wallowing in the mire.

I know many denominations teach and preach eternal security, and in good conscience I cannot believe this doctrine. There are too many scriptures that **teach**

132

against eternal security. When a person dies in a backslidden condition, they **do not go to heaven**. Please **search the scriptures** for yourself and **know the truth**.

Verse seven talks about men and women who desire to be ministers and teachers when they really do not know what they believe. To be a teacher or preacher, one must be **rooted and grounded in the Word of God**. When you occupy a place of authority in the church, you **stand responsible before God** for every soul under you. There are some in the church today that change their beliefs with every new thing that comes along. The Word teaches us that **to be unstable is to be out of God's will**. Know the truth of the Word, stand upon it, and do not be swayed by men's doctrine.

Make no mistake about this one thing: after you receive salvation, this in no way gives you a license to sin. There are those who will try to teach that after you repent and accept Jesus Christ as your Saviour, you are free from sin no matter how you live or what you do. Wrong, wrong, wrong. **Salvation does not excuse you from being able to sin.** Listen to what I am saying, there are no saved idol worshipers. **We cannot stay saved and be a liar**, a thief, **an adulterer**, a fornicator, **a drunkard or many other things**. The scriptures below give a list of those who will not enter into heaven.

Matthew 7:21-23

> *21 Not every one that saith unto me, Lord, Lord, shall enter into the kingdom of heaven; but he that*

doeth the will of my Father which is in heaven.

²² Many will say to me in that day, Lord, Lord, have we not prophesied in thy name? and in thy name have cast out devils? and in thy name done many wonderful works?

²³ And then will I profess unto them, I never knew you: depart from me, ye that work iniquity.

Romans 1:18-32

¹⁸ For the wrath of God is revealed from heaven against all ungodliness and unrighteousness of men, who hold the truth in unrighteousness;

¹⁹ Because that which may be known of God is manifest in them; for God hath shewed it unto them.

²⁰ For the invisible things of him from the creation of the world are clearly seen, being understood by the things that are made, even his eternal power and Godhead; so that they are without excuse:

²¹ Because that, when they knew God, they glorified him not as God, neither were thankful; but became vain in their imaginations, and their foolish heart was darkened.

²² Professing themselves to be wise, they became fools,

²³ And changed the glory of the uncorruptible God into an image made like to corruptible man, and to birds, and fourfooted beasts, and creeping things.

²⁴ Wherefore God also gave them up to uncleanness

through the lusts of their own hearts, to dishonour their own bodies between themselves:

²⁵ Who changed the truth of God into a lie, and worshipped and served the creature more than the Creator, who is blessed for ever. Amen.

²⁶ For this cause God gave them up unto vile affections: for even their women did change the natural use into that which is against nature:

²⁷ And likewise also the men, leaving the natural use of the woman, burned in their lust one toward another; men with men working that which is unseemly, and receiving in themselves that recompence of their error which was meet.

²⁸ And even as they did not like to retain God in their knowledge, God gave them over to a reprobate mind, to do those things which are not convenient;

²⁹ Being filled with all unrighteousness, fornication, wickedness, covetousness, maliciousness; full of envy, murder, debate, deceit, malignity; whisperers,

³⁰ Backbiters, haters of God, despiteful, proud, boasters, inventors of evil things, disobedient to parents,

³¹ Without understanding, covenantbreakers, without natural affection, implacable, unmerciful:

³² Who knowing the judgment of God, that they which commit such things are worthy of death, not only do the same, but have pleasure in them that do them.

1 Corinthians 6:9-10

⁹ Know ye not that the unrighteous shall not inherit the kingdom of God? Be not deceived: neither fornicators, nor idolaters, nor adulterers, nor effeminate, nor abusers of themselves with mankind, ¹⁰ Nor thieves, nor covetous, nor drunkards, nor revilers, nor extortioners, shall inherit the kingdom of God.

Galatians 5:19-21

¹⁹ Now the works of the flesh are manifest, which are these; Adultery, fornication, uncleanness, lasciviousness,
²⁰ Idolatry, witchcraft, hatred, variance, emulations, wrath, strife, seditions, heresies,
²¹ Envyings, murders, drunkenness, revellings, and such like: of the which I tell you before, as I have also told you in time past, that they which do such things shall not inherit the kingdom of God.

Colossians 3:5-6

⁵ Mortify therefore your members which are upon the earth; fornication, uncleanness, inordinate affection, evil concupiscence, and covetousness, which is idolatry:
⁶ For which things' sake the wrath of God cometh

on the children of disobedience:

Revelation 21:8

> *But the fearful, and unbelieving, and the abominable, and murderers, and whoremongers, and sorcerers, and idolaters, and all liars, shall have their part in the lake which burneth with fire and brimstone: which is the second death.*

Please take note that by doing the above sins, you were condemned to a devil's hell before you repented and accepted Jesus Christ as your Saviour. Also remember that if they **condemned you before you were saved**, they will also **condemn you after you are saved**, if you continue to do them. Our God is no respecter of persons. **Sin is sin and sin will send your soul to a real devil's hell** …

You will want your own copy of this exciting new study coming soon at www.ParadiseGospelPress.com.

www.ingramcontent.com/pod-product-compliance
Lightning Source LLC
Chambersburg PA
CBHW060907280326
41934CB00007B/1226